WITHDRAWN

Common Reading Programs
Going Beyond the Book

Jodi Levine Laufgraben, Author & Editor

D1568371

National Resource Center for The First-Year Experience® & Students in Transition, University of South Carolina, 2006

Cite as:

Laufgraben, J. L. (2006). *Common reading programs: Going beyond the book* (Monograph No. 44). Columbia, SC: University of South Carolina, National Resource Center for The First-Year Experience and Students in Transition.

Sample chapter citation:

Andersen, C. F. (2006). Assessing common reading programs. In J. L. Laufgraben, *Common reading programs: Going beyond the book* (Monograph No. 44, pp. 75-91). Columbia, SC: University of South Carolina, National Resource Center for The First-Year Experience and Students in Transition.

ISBN-10 1-889271-53-5
ISBN-13 978-1-889-27153-8

The First-Year Experience® is a service mark of the University of South Carolina. A license may be granted upon written request to use the term "The First-Year Experience." This license is not transferable without written approval of the University of South Carolina.

Additional copies of this monograph may be obtained from the National Resource Center for The First-Year Experience and Students in Transition, University of South Carolina, 1728 College Street, Columbia, SC 29208. Telephone (803) 777-6029. Fax (803) 777-4699.

Special gratitude is expressed to Tracy L. Skipper, Editorial Projects Coordinator, for project management and copyediting; to Barbara F. Tobolowsky, Associate Director, and Michael Abel, Editorial Assistant, for copyediting and proofing; to Inge Kutt Lewis, Editor, for proofing; and to Erin M. Morris, Graphic Artist, for layout and design.

Photo Credits: Keith McGraw, University of South Carolina, pp. vii, 1, 11, 19, 65, 75; Erin M. Morris, University of South Carolina, pp. 33, 93; Temple University Photography Department, p. 45

Laufgraben, Jodi Levine, 1966-
 Common reading programs : going beyond the book / Jodi Levine Laufgraben, author and editor.
     p. cm. -- (The first-year experience monograph series ; no. 44)
 Includes bibliographical references.
 ISBN-13: 978-1-889271-53-8
 ISBN-10: 1-889271-53-5
1. College student development programs--United States. 2. College freshman--Books and reading--United States. I. National Resource Center for the First-Year Experience & Students in Transition (University of South Carolina) II. Title. III. Series.
 LB2343.4.L38 2006
 378.1'98--dc22
                              2006008107

Contents

Tables, Boxes, & Campus Cases

Foreword

Mary Stuart Hunter

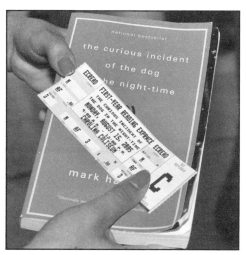

When the University of South Carolina began our summer reading program in 1994, I knew that the newly created program had the potential to do several things I believed were important. It would create a common experience for many of our new students; it would incorporate an academic component into welcome week activities; and it would bring faculty and staff from across our campus together for a common purpose. Having been involved with planning and decision making for the first-year reading program on my own campus for a number of years now, I have seen the powerful possibilities for the program unfold as it develops, expands, and encompasses an ever-widening variety of components. Each year, the shared experience in and of itself is a highlight for me and, I am sure, for many others. There is an electric buzz on campus each fall as the new class comes together en masse with hundreds of faculty and staff to learn from one another through discussion on the book of the year.

Common reading programs are not a new phenomenon in American higher education, and we never thought we were pioneers with our summer reading program at the University of South Carolina. As early as 1965, *The College Student's Handbook* by Lass and Wilson reported that "more and more colleges are asking or requiring their freshmen to read one or several books during the summer before they come to college. Then during orientation period or the early part of the first semester, discussions of this material are led by faculty or upperclassmen" (pp. 9-10). No doubt, many campuses had similar programs over the years. More recently, Internet technology has allowed us to have easier access to information on what exists beyond our own campus. I have encouraged my colleagues here at the National Resource Center for The First-Year Experience and Students in Transition to develop resources on common and summer reading programs for our web site so that higher educators everywhere will have access to information on these programs. I have seen the lists of campuses with programs grow with each passing year, and I have seen the list of books used by these programs lengthen as well. In recent years, an increasing number of publishers have exhibited at our conferences and offered conference participants complimentary copies of books to consider for common reading programs. Despite this increased attention, the literature base on common reading programs remains extremely small. So when Jodi Laufgraben approached our Center about developing a monograph on this topic, we were happy to support her efforts. This is, indeed, a topic that I support with enthusiasm. What I did not anticipate was that I would learn so much by reading the manuscript.

The authors provide a rich, idea-laden resource for readers who seek guidance for creating new common reading programs or who want simply to enhance existing initiatives. Specific chapters present clear and well-developed guidance on all aspects of common reading programs from beginning to end. They provide a solid rationale and offer examples of specific goals for a program, describe a long list of potential program components, and suggest ideas for planning and promoting a program. Additionally, suggestions are shared for selecting a text, planning events and activities for the program, and developing classroom pedagogy surrounding the text. A comprehensive chapter on assessing common reading programs ensures that readers have guidance on how to continuously improve their campus programs. As I read this manuscript, I was inspired by the resourcefulness and creativity of colleagues administering common reading programs at colleges and universities across the country. The tables, charts, and lists included throughout the monograph will be of tremendous value to you as you consider the efforts on your own campus.

When I finished reading the manuscript, excitement and anticipation grew within me. I felt a strong urge to gather with the other members of our planning committee to get to work on further improving our own program at the University of South Carolina. As I write this, I am anxious for the publication date to arrive so that I can share a copy with each member of our campus committee so that they, too, will be able to read about the many components of wonderful programs in place on other campuses. Knowing the positive influence that a common reading experience can have on a campus, I am confident that you will be inspired by the possibilities shared in this monograph. Happy reading!

Mary Stuart Hunter
Director, National Resource Center
for The First-Year Experience and Students in Transition

Reference

Lass, A. H., & Wilson, E. S. (1965). *The college student's handbook*. New York: D. White.

Introduction

Common Reading Programs
Going Beyond the Book

Jodi Levine Laufgraben

First-year reading experiences are increasingly common on college campuses, but little has been written on what these programs are and on the extent to which they achieve academic objectives. A simple definition is that common reading programs are educationally purposeful programs that engage students in a variety of in- and out-of-class academic and social experiences. Despite this definition, a misconception exists that these programs involve little more than selecting a book and asking or requiring students to read it. In fact, many common reading programs do consist of students reading an assigned book over the summer and then discussing it with their peers and teachers when they arrive on campus for the start of their first college year. Yet, other programs have grown to include library exhibits, film series, theatrical performances, and grant-funded faculty development experiences. As such, these programs move beyond seeing the common reading experience as an orientation activity. Thus, a question this monograph explores is "How do campuses move beyond the book as an orientation event to create an ongoing and engaging academic initiative for students?"

Successful programs are broadly defined for purposes of this monograph as programs that (a) have clearly articulated goals and plan activities in alignment with these goals, (b) build partnerships across campus, (c) move beyond isolated efforts to sustained initiatives embedded in the campus culture, (d) are innovative and creative, and (e) use assessment for program improvement. Colleagues at several colleges and universities that have been successful in creating such conditions were invited to submit narratives of their programs to be used as examples in this monograph. Their submissions became the body of evidence used in good part to compile the lists of goals, characteristics, and activities of common reading programs. Web sites of other programs and e-mail exchanges with colleagues directing common reading initiatives provided additional, valuable insights into innovative work.

This monograph describes the rationale for common reading programs along with goals and potential outcomes. It also describes the primary elements of common reading programs including: (a) planning and promoting programs, (b) designing events and activities, (c) selecting the reading, (d) connecting common readings to the curriculum, and (e) assessing the program. Chapter 1 outlines the goals and purposes of common reading programs. Chapter 2 focuses on types of common reading programs and the primary components of such programs. Creating and promoting common reading programs, including the resources needed to support them, is the subject of chapter 3. Chapter 4 includes advice and examples of how different institutions approach the task of selecting the book.

Chapter 5 offers advice on planning ancillary events and activities for the common reading, while chapter 6 takes up strategies for incorporating common reading programs into the classroom, including a brief overview of the pedagogies that can promote active and collaborative learning. In chapter 7, Catherine Andersen describes some basic assessment principles with examples of assessment from several common reading programs. The monograph concludes with a summary of themes from across the chapters and a discussion of trends and future directions. In addition, text boxes located in each chapter highlight specific designs, structures, or activities of several established programs and provide examples for other educators to consider as they build, sustain, and improve their common reading efforts.

Several people were responsible for the writing of this monograph. I would like to thank Stuart Hunter for asking me what I might like to focus on for my next project and to Tracy Skipper for keeping me on task and encouraging me to move ahead with this project. I am especially grateful to Liz Clark, Nancy Spann, Donnelle Graham, Zaide Pixley, Diane Seuss, Catherine Andersen, Stephen Braye, Kristen diNovi, and Carrie Linder for crafting the case studies on their programs that provided the rich, descriptive examples placed throughout this book. A special thank you as well, to other colleagues who spent time via e-mail or phone educating me about the best practices of their common reading programs. I greatly appreciate the contributions Chris Dennis and Catherine Andersen made to chapters in this monograph. It is a privilege to call you colleagues and friends. As with all my writing projects, I am especially grateful to my Temple colleagues and my family for supporting my work and helping me find the time to write and edit.

All of us involved with this monograph hope it will help educators design and improve their common reading experiences. We see this book as a starting point for on-campus discussions about the goals and values of reading programs and for broader conversations about promoting student success.

Chapter One

The Rationale and Goals of Common Reading Programs

Common reading initiatives are often very similar in purpose and design, regardless of campus size or institutional type. Participants in the First-Year Experience Listserv succinctly stated those purposes: "to provide a common academic experience for all first-year students and to strengthen the academic atmosphere of the institution from the first day the student arrives on campus" (Patterson, 2002, p. 8). Important and related goals were connecting students to their peers and teachers and getting students involved in campus activities. Many programs start with a desire to "intellectualize" orientation or the beginning undergraduate experience for entering students and then develop into academic programs with cocurricular and curricular components that involve teachers, students, and members of the campus community in a shared learning experience.

Rationale for Common Reading Programs

Many campuses begin common reading programs with the intent of enhancing students' transition to college and the goal of increasing student success. Narrowly defined, first-year student success involves completion of the courses in the first year of college and persistence to the second year. Upcraft, Gardner, and Barefoot (2005), however, note that most campuses extend the definition of first-year student success to include (a) developing intellectual competence, (b) establishing and maintaining interpersonal relationships, (c) exploring identity development, (d) developing multicultural awareness, and (e) developing civic responsibility. Common reading programs contribute to student success because they emphasize reading as an intellectual skill central to student achievement and promote learning with and from others. Many of the books selected for the common reading experience explore themes (e.g., identity, gender, race, ethnicity, civic responsibility) that contribute to students' academic and social development and can be explored from multiple points of view. Asking students to read a selected book, however, is not enough to make the claim that a common reading initiative promotes student success. Common reading initiatives need to be structured with the broader goal of student success at the center, but more importantly, need to (a) model academic behaviors, (b) set expectations for student success, (c) foster involvement, and (d) promote more meaningful learning.

Model Academic Behaviors

By establishing an intellectual community early in a student's tenure on campus, common reading programs model important academic behaviors for students. They also enhance students' ability to read for understanding, raise questions, and listen to diverse points of view. Pedagogically, many common reading programs revolve around small-group discussions, which emphasize critical analysis of a text and may later help students formulate written arguments and support claims about the text. Finally, these programs allow students to draw parallels between what they read and personal experiences, an important activity that engages students in academic learning.

When the selected book is controversial, such as the University of North Carolina at Chapel Hill's 2002 choice of *Approaching the Qur'án: The Early Revelations* (a translation of the early suras or the short, hymnic chapters at the end of the Qur'án), additional opportunities for modeling academic behaviors, such as academic freedom, exist. Through participation in discussions, students come to better understand diverse perspectives and conflicting opinions. Students see the practice of academic freedom and the potential of open debate. The controversy that might emerge from the selection of a particular book teaches not only successful academic behaviors but also important civic values. If alternate viewpoints are not allowed to be expressed, an important teaching moment is lost.

Set Expectations for Student Success

The goals and activities of common reading programs are also consistent with the types of environments that promote student learning. Students' expectations of college shape their behavior, which in turn affects their academic performance and social adjustment to college life (Kuh, 2005). Kuh notes the gap between students' expectations and their actual experiences and suggests colleges *"get to students early"* (p. 99, emphasis added) to help narrow this gap. Students need to hear early and often what it takes to succeed in college. Further, Kuh cautions: "Low expectations almost always produce low levels of engagement" (p. 106). A common reading program sends the message—early in a student's transition—that reading and discourse are expected in college. When teachers incorporate the common reading in classes, they reinforce the importance of reading and model ways to discuss and write about a book.

Common reading programs also help set expectations for students by highlighting important intellectual skills and abilities, including:

- Effective oral, visual, and written communication skills

- The ability to interpret and evaluate information from a variety of sources

- The ability to understand and work within complex systems and with diverse groups

- The ability to transform information into knowledge and knowledge into judgment and action

Moreover, such programs help students understand that reading, critical thinking, discussion, and other activities are expected in college and contribute to learning. For first-year students, reading programs can help transform orientation from a primarily social or advising-and-registration activity to a time of academic engagement with students, faculty, and the greater campus community.

Foster Involvement

Successful common reading programs are also grounded in the literature on student involvement and learning. Common reading programs merge the curricular and cocurricular components of college and reinforce the message that learning occurs both inside and outside the classroom. In planning a common reading program, campuses need to consider the environment necessary to encourage student participation and recognition of the educational value of their involvement. While some colleges and universities require student participation in a common reading, on most campuses the expectation is that students will choose to read the book and then participate actively in common reading events. For many students, "Should I read it?" is one of the first decisions they make about getting involved on campus. Of course, campuses want students to answer "Yes," and certain conditions will make that answer more likely. Kuh, Douglas, Lund, and Ramin-Gyurnek (1994) outlined nine institutional conditions that encourage students to make use of out-of-class activities to enhance learning. These conditions include:

1. Clear, coherent, and consistently expressed educational purposes

2. An institutional philosophy that embraces a holistic view of talent development

3. Complementary institutional policies and practices congruent with students' characteristics and needs

4. High, clear expectations for student performance

5. Use of effective teaching approaches

6. Systematic assessment of student performance and institutional environments, policies, and practices

7. Ample opportunities for student involvement in educationally purposeful out-of-class activities

8. Human-scale settings characterized by ethics of membership and care

9. An ethos of learning that pervades all aspects of the institution. (p. iv)

Common reading programs incorporate many of these conditions. For example, reading programs often include among their educational goals promoting reading, debate, discussion, and critical thinking. Reading programs offer diverse opportunities for involvement from small-group discussions to book readings to lectures with faculty. Activities also include opportunities for creativity such as theatrical or musical performances, essay contests, or art exhibits. From the outset, students are encouraged to read a book and to discuss it with peers, teachers, and other members of the college community in an environment that promotes community and respect. Students are expected to share their views and to respect the viewpoints of others. When common reading programs involve students, faculty, and the greater campus or surrounding community in the intellectual activity of reading and discussion, students become engaged in a campus-wide learning environment.

Kuh (2005) stresses the importance of offering ways for students to spend time with each other. By design, common reading programs engage students in educationally purposeful activities with their peers. A common reading program also balances academic and social activities, particularly for new students. Bringing students together over lunch or dinner to discuss a book offers a casual setting for students to get to know each other while maintaining an academic focus. Common reading programs also promote peer engagement by helping students understand the value of talking about academic matters outside the classroom. When a reading selection is discussed in class and students also have the opportunity to attend related events with peers and teachers outside classes, they see how the curricular and extracurricular components of college contribute to their overall learning experiences.

According to Terenzini, Springer, Pascarella, and Nora (1993), involving students in both in-class and out-of-class activities can impact their cognitive development, including critical thinking. Student interactions with peers and faculty also positively impact cognitive gains. In a study of the impact of course taking, formal classroom experiences, and out-of-class experiences on critical thinking in the first-year of college, Terenzini et al. found that "the number of hours students spent studying and the number of non-assigned books read during the year were positively related to gains in critical thinking" (p. 9). Because common reading programs bridge both the in-class and out-of-class dimensions of learning, they are one vehicle for enhancing critical thinking in college.

As summarized by Terenzini et al. (1993), gains in student development depend on a variety of student experiences. Common reading programs go beyond "a book" and promote discussion, creativity, imagination, and critical thinking. Students can talk about the book in the campus dining hall over lunch with their friends, raise issues with a faculty member during a small group discussion, or view a film to better understand the historical context of a book. They can write an essay analyzing critical plot elements and then ask the visiting author why he or she made those decisions about the plot.

Promote More Meaningful Learning

Involvement and more meaningful learning are closely related and interconnected conditions for student success. Barr and Tagg (1995) describe a learning paradigm that shifts from a traditional instructional model of transferring knowledge from teacher to students (i.e., having a professor "teach" a book) to creating "environments and experiences that bring students to discover and construct knowledge for themselves, to make students members of communities of learners that make discoveries and solve problems" (p. 12). When students read a common book and share their perspectives with peers and teachers, they are given the opportunity to engage in the type of higher-order, integrative, and reflective learning Barr and Tagg describe. Students are able to make judgments about the validity of what they read, discuss these ideas with others whose views may differ from their own, and consider alternative perspectives. Students can connect what they read to what they learned previously and to the new knowledge they are acquiring in college. When students experience this type of learning environment, they are the "chief agent" in the learning process and are empowered to discover and create new knowledge around what they have read.

When Temple students read *Fast Food Nation*, Eric Schlosser's close-up look at the fast food industry, they not only engaged in a discussion of the nutritional value of fast food but also of the economic and social impact of the fast food industry on society. For some students, considering the impact of their fast food purchases on the wages of some of America's poorest residents led them to question their devotion to their industry favorite. When Temple selected *Lies My Teacher Told Me: Everything Your American History Textbook Got Wrong*—a survey of 12 leading high school American history textbooks—participants in summer reading discussions and attendees of the author's talk had to consider author James Lowen's research methods and whether the way he described events was more historically accurate than the way those events have been described in high school texts or popular culture. In both cases, students become active participants in knowledge construction rather than passive recipients of an already-defined body of content.

Reading, by itself, can also promote more meaningful learning. According to results from the National Survey of Student Engagement (NSSE, 2004), students who spend more time reading outside class score higher on the deeper-learning scale. Thirty-one percent of students who scored in the top quartile indicated they read five or more books for their own personal enjoyment or academic enrichment during the school year compared to only 17% in the lower quartile.

In his introductory remarks to the 2004 annual report of the National Survey of Student Engagement, Kuh reminded colleges and universities that the term "student success" is more than a buzz word and that they need to take action if they want to realize it (NSSE, 2004). For example, he suggests that institutions should "create *pathways to engagement* that are clearly marked, so that students can more easily find their way to become involved in purposeful activities" (p. 5, original emphasis). A common reading program can be an early and purposeful activity that illuminates that path for students by modeling the type of learning and engagement that promotes their learning and success.

Goals and Purposes of Common Reading Programs

The goals for common reading programs should pertain to all those involved in these initiatives. Frequently, the goals for students are the most prominent. For example, by providing a common reading program, institutions may seek to encourage reading among students, create a sense of community on campus, promote discussion, set academic expectations for students, provide a shared intellectual experience, and encourage cross-disciplinary dialogues. Faculty also benefit from participation if the programs increase opportunities for interactions with students and colleagues from other departments, offer practice facilitating dialogues, and encourage interdisciplinary writing assignments. Similarly, institutions may envision goals for the larger campus or community, which may include creating dialogue among students, faculty, staff, and the community; promoting the institution's resources and programs to the community; and introducing students to community resources, such as the public library.

Successful programs are designed to incorporate most or all of these goals. At Miami University, the Summer Reading Program exemplifies "those activities we most value as a community: critical engagement with ideas; close interaction among faculty, staff, and students; and reading, listening, talking, and learning as important characteristics of active, responsible citizenship" (Miami University of Ohio, n.d.). To underscore the importance of program goals, common reading initiatives are often described as students' "first assignment" in college. For example, Miami's web site clearly states the rationale for their program:

> Participation in the Summer Reading Program is your first assignment as a university student. Your willingness to take the assignment seriously and to participate actively in group discussions in August may have important influences on your subsequent achievements as a Miami Student.

Creating community is an important goal of many common reading programs. If the program is part of new student orientation, the reading selection usually provides opportunities for student-faculty interaction during orientation. Faculty-led discussion groups bring small groups of students together with a teacher and their peers to explore and discuss the major themes of the selected work. Members of the university community may gather at planned events such as book signings, author-led discussions, readings, performances, and lectures. The experience with a common reading program at Kalamazoo College demonstrates how this sense of community emerges:

> We have found this process…moves individuals out of their habitual "corners"—an admissions counselor finds herself engaged in a discussion of the book with a history professor; a member of the Counseling Center staff and the basketball coach spend an hour and a half with a group of incoming students discussing South American politics. Irreplaceable new alliances are formed. (Z. Pixley, personal communication, August 2004)

The First-Year Reading Experience at the University of South Carolina began after the then Associate Provost and Dean for Undergraduate Affairs spoke with faculty, students, and staff about the University's approach to welcoming new students. Students commented that they wanted more common academic experiences and the opportunity for ungraded contact with faculty (C. Linder, personal communication, August 2004). The program started with four goals: (a) begin Welcome Week with an academic focus, (b) allow students to experience a college-level discussion in a non-threatening atmosphere, (c) create a common academic experience for a portion of the University's incoming students, and (d) give students an opportunity to interact with faculty outside the classroom. Such responsiveness to student concerns is an important step in helping them find community on campus.

Often, common reading programs emerge from existing first-year experience efforts and become part of a broader effort to promote student success. At LaGuardia Community College, the common reading program aims to welcome students to the college while also helping to connect students with diverse backgrounds and abilities. Campus Case 1.1 describes the goals and expectations of LaGuardia Community College's common reading programs.

Campus Case 1.1

Program Goals
LaGuardia Community College
J. Elizabeth Clark

LaGuardia Community College has an academic-year common reading program that began in 2001 as part of the first-year experience initiative. The College was interested in providing students with an immediate and personal connection to the college. Through the common reading, LaGuardia aims to create a greater sense of community among students and to provide an introduction to intellectual life at the College.

Full-time, part-time, day and evening students create a lively, bubbling campus of 12,000 students who cross campus at all times of the day and night. As a large, multicultural, urban, commuter campus, LaGuardia's students enter the college at widely varying points in their academic trajectory. Eighty percent of LaGuardia's students enter needing some type of developmental coursework, and 34% enter the college as non-matriculated students in English-as-a-Second-Language (ESL) programs. Still others enter needing no remediation, enroll in the honors program, and take a traditional course of study. The common reading program has become one of the central programs in LaGuardia's first-year experience, welcoming and introducing students to the intellectual life of the College while offering a means of connection among their disparate experiences.

The program relies on sharing the idea with students that their education and success is important to the entire college community. Accordingly, the campus community comes together to celebrate students' beginnings in college and to extend conversations around the common reading throughout the year. The program introduces students to books—and when possible—to living authors. This is a key experience in students' intellectual development as they come to recognize earning a degree as more than a "hoop" they must go through before entering the workforce.

LaGuardia has been building on the success of the common reading from the very first year. In the beginning, the common reading was mainly a facet of Student Opening Sessions. Over time, the program has slowly expanded its cocurricular offerings, turning the common reading into a full-year experience with programs, discussion groups, and other related activities scheduled throughout the year.

As programs evolve, goals may change or expand. After four years, the Common Reading Program at Appalachian State University was expanded into a community-wide program called "If All of Watauga Read the Same Book." The program aims to: (a) enhance the academic climate for first-year students; (b) provide a common intellectual experience; and (c) enhance a sense of community among students, faculty, and staff. Appalachian State added the community piece to build on the existing connection between Watauga County and the University, involve people of all ages in a shared reading experience, and enhance the community readers' appreciation of literature. A community committee consisting of representatives from Appalachian State University, the Watauga County Library, Caldwell Community College (Watauga campus), and Watauga County Schools plans community events around the selected book (N. Spann & D. Graham, personal communication, December 2004).

Many common reading programs share similar goals, and these goals are often closely aligned with broader objectives such as promoting student success and creating a sense of community on campus. Established programs—and those perhaps best positioned to be supported and sustained over time—however, have adapted goals, structures, and activities to fit the unique student, faculty, and institutional culture of their campuses.

Conclusion

When developing a common reading program, an important first step is considering the goals, purposes, and intended outcomes for participants. The goals for the common reading program inform all other decisions about the project, and events and activities should be designed to achieve the intended outcomes. Programs should aim to reach a broad audience, and a common reading initiative should be developed as an experience not only for students but also for faculty, staff, and members of the community. By focusing on such a broad audience, these initiatives have a greater chance to raise expectations for students and promote learning and success.

Chapter Two

Components and Types of Common Reading Programs

Since there is not an established literature base on common reading programs, no single, best definition of these initiatives exists. Programs can vary in type, expectations, scope, and size. Some campuses select a single book for new students to read during orientation, while other campuses may provide students with a reader consisting of multiple reading selections organized around a theme. The "common" component involves a targeted audience asked to read the same text(s) in a defined period of time so that participants can engage in an academic discourse about those texts. The program might require entering first-year students to read a selected book over the summer prior to arriving on campus, or the program might invite all members of the college or university, as well as the surrounding community, to read a common book during the fall or spring terms. This chapter focuses on the typical components of first-year reading experiences (see Box 2.1) and describes different types of reading initiatives.

Components of Common Reading Programs

The Reading

Most common reading programs are organized around a selected work of fiction or non-fiction. Some programs, like the First-Year Reading Experience at the University of South Carolina, have used classics such as F. Scott Fitzgerald's *The Great*

Box 2.1

Characteristics of Common Reading Experiences

- Involve an assigned reading of one or more books or reading selections
- Are academically oriented
- Promote reading, critical thinking, and discussion skills
- Bring students, faculty, and staff together around a common intellectual activity
- Focus on a theme generated from the selected work
- Incorporate a range of activities around the selected work
- Have shared program leadership among academic and student affairs or multiple offices and individuals across a campus

---

Gatsby or Ernest Hemingway's *The Sun Also Rises*. Plays may also be selected. In 1999, entering first-year students at the University of Pennsylvania read *Copenhagen* by Michael Frayn, a play that reimagines the mysterious wartime meeting between two Nobel laureates to discuss the atomic bomb. Other programs ask students to read a collection of poems or selected articles, typically organized into a reader around a theme such as transition to college or multicultural awareness. The type of book or readings selected may be influenced by a variety of factors, including but not limited to goals for the common reading project, mission of the college or university, local or regional topics of interest, current events, or popular culture. Other books are selected because they raise themes relevant to first-year students and their transition to college such as coming of age, relationships, family, diversity, or self-exploration. Selecting the reading is discussed in greater detail in chapter 4.

Academic Focus

By design, common reading programs promote reading and discussion, two activities central to learning in college. Whether coordinated by academic affairs or student affairs, there is usually significant involvement of faculty as well as other members of the campus community. Common reading programs embedded in new student orientation are promoted as an academic activity designed to help students make the transition to academic discourse and the intellectual life of the campus. For example, the University of North Carolina (UNC) at Chapel Hill refers to its Summer Reading Program as an "academic icebreaker" (UNC News Services, 2005). While on many campuses the common reading program is considered a voluntary or non-credit bearing assignment, the reading may also be incorporated into courses. Connecting reading programs to the curriculum is discussed in chapter 6.

Skill Development

In addition to academic enrichment, many common reading programs aim to promote specific habits of learning, including reading, critical thinking, and discussion. The selected books often are interdisciplinary in nature to allow conversations across subject areas. Many common reading programs include small group discussion sessions with a faculty member or peer leader, as well as a featured lecture or talk, often delivered by the author or a scholarly expert on the book or writer. This discussion allows students to explore perceptions of what they read with others and provides them with an important opportunity to examine a text from multiple viewpoints. When the selected reading is incorporated into a course, such as college composition or first-year seminar, additional occasions for ongoing discussion and debate arise, along with opportunities to write about the reading.

Theme

Before or after a book or readings are selected, the common reading program may take on a theme around which resource materials and activities are planned. The theme is useful for organizing lecture series, discussion sessions, essay contests, and other intellectual activities, but it can also be used to prepare resource materials, such as discussion questions or related reading lists. The committee and project planners often engage in their own book discussion and, as a by-product of their decision making, identify themes and issues that can later be discussed by students and teachers. These themes are further delineated when the common reading planners create announcements about the book and develop resource materials. An overarching theme for the selection can help tie perspectives together and help students understand the rationale behind a choice. These themes are then interpreted and explored from different disciplinary perspectives. For the 2004-2005 Common Book program, Otterbein College students read *The Eagle's Shadow: Why America Fascinates and Infuriates the World*, written by Mark Hertsgaard following his trip around the world to gather perceptions about America from people in 15 countries. The theme for the year was "Trading Places: The U.S. as Others See Us." The year prior, the theme was "Dreams and Disappointments," and students read Anthony Grooms' *Bombingham*, a novel depicting the events of the Civil Rights Movement and the Vietnam War through the heightened perspective of a narrator who struggles to find the meaning of his role in both events. Other past selections and themes from Otterbein College are included in Table 2.1.

With almost any selected book or reading, there is typically no limit to the issues that can be explored. The common reading committee and faculty planners may identify a theme or set of issues to be explored around the reading(s), but this a starting point and should not limit the tone and scope of conversations and learning activities. Students and faculty bring different experiences, backgrounds, skills, and interests to the college environment. The curricular component of a common reading

Table 2.1
Past Books and Themes, Otterbein College

Year	Theme	Selection
2004-2005	Trading Places: The U.S. As Others See US	Mark Hertsgaard, *The Eagle's Shadow: Why America Fascinates and Infuriates the World*
2003-2004	Dreams and Disappointments	Anthony Grooms, *Bombingham*
2002-2003	Change. Not So Easy	Ruth L. Ozeki, *My Year of Meats*
2001-2002	Making Contact	Mary Doria Russell, *The Sparrow*
2000-2001	Selves and Stories, Disguise, and Disclosure	Helen Fremont, *After Long Silence*
1999-2000	Building Walls, Creating Doors	Alex Kotlowitz, *There Are No Children Here*
1998-1999	Legacies	Sharyn McCrumb, *She Walks These Hills*
1997-1998	Conscience & Courage: Personal Landscapes	Scott Russell Sanders, *The Paradise of Bombs*
1996-1997	Educating for Community: Growing Apart and Staying Together	Gus Lee, *China Boy*
1995-1996	Culture, Conflict, and Community	Anna Deavere Smith, *Fires in the Mirror: Crown Heights, Brooklyn and Other Identities*

program should embrace these differences while creating welcoming settings for shared exploration of a reading. For example, when Temple University first-year students read James Lowen's *Lies My Teacher Told Me: Everything Your American History Textbook Got Wrong*, students in a history class discussed different ethnic and racial perspectives on certain events in American history, students in a business course discussed the economics of the textbook industry, and students in a first-year seminar discussed research methods and sources for verifying textbook facts.

Activities

Common reading programs feature more than an assigned reading. When asked to read a book, particularly if the reading program is not required and the book will not be incorporated or assigned as part of classwork, students will often ask, "I read the book, now what?" Many entering college students had summer reading assignments or required book lists when they were in high school. In many instances, these summer readings became their first assignments when they arrived for the start of the school year. Based on their past summer reading experiences, some students arrive at college having left high school environments where they write papers, prepare presentations, or take quizzes or tests on what they were required to read.

Summer reading programs, however, often promote reading for the "sake of reading"—i.e., for personal growth, intellectual development, and for shared conversation. Activities provide students the opportunity to come together to discuss what they read and to raise and answer questions about the work. They can promote discourse (e.g., readings, lectures, talks by the authors, or discussion sessions) or creativity (e.g., musical performances, essay contests, or art exhibits). For example, the common reading experience at LaGuardia Community College features a variety of activities beginning with discussions held during Student Opening Sessions—the welcome events held prior to the start of the semester—and continuing with events held throughout the semester such as movies, lectures, plays, and an author visit. Community events include theater productions, readings, and panel discussions. On some campuses, activities include the local community. When Appalachian State selected Ernest Gaines' *A Lesson Before Dying*—the story of a man condemned to die for a crime he did not commit and the young man who visits him—Caldwell Community College's Watauga Campus sponsored a panel discussion entitled "The Death Penalty: Is It Fair?" Panelists included local attorneys, an Appalachian State University criminal justice professor, a local psychologist, and an ethics and philosophy professor from Caldwell Community College. For other selections, community events have included discussions at the public library and exhibits at the high school library.

Shared Leadership

Common reading programs are designed to promote community and should be planned collaboratively. Many programs, even if the original impetus comes from a single unit or division, typically develop out of a collaborative, cross-campus effort. On many campuses, the book is selected by a committee that includes faculty, administrators, students, and staff. When the common reading initiative is intended primarily as an orientation or new student welcome event, first-year experience directors or staff, librarians, housing and residence life personnel, and orientation leadership are typically involved. At Bowling Green State University, a committee of faculty, administration, staff, and students oversee the common reading program. The committee includes the director of English Composition, representation from the learning communities programs, and members of the First-Year Experience Office. The first-year experience librarian chairs the committee.

Types of Common Reading Programs

There is no prescribed typology of common reading programs, and types of programs may vary on an individual campus from year to year based on the selected work, goals, intended audiences, and planned time line for the project. Programs also vary in terms of timing (i.e., during orientation or throughout the academic term), delivery (i.e., cocurricular vs. curriculum-based), and audience (i.e., the college community or the larger local community).

An *orientation-based common reading program* targets entering students. New students are asked or required to read the selected text(s) prior to arriving on campus for the start of the school year. In many cases, the students come to campus in the summer for orientation or registration and advising and learn about the common reading program at that time. They may be given a copy of the book(s) along with a reading guide. When students return to campus in late August or early September, they participate in a range of activities organized around the reading. Common reading events may end during orientation or activities may extend into the first semester or across the entire year. This type of program, as an academic component of orientation, can be administered by academic affairs, student affairs, or as a collaborative effort. Campus Case 2.1 describes the Summer Common Reading Program at Kalamazoo College, which coincides with new student orientation.

In-semester programs engage students in a common reading program throughout the first academic term. These initiatives may be curricular or cocurricular. A curricular-based effort may link a common reading to a particular course or the general education program, while a cocurricular program asks students to read a book and participate in activities not linked to a particular academic requirement. The program can target entering students or all students, who are given a copy of the book or made aware of its availability for purchase on campus. Activities are planned around the reading and continue across the semester or quarter.

A *year-long program* uses events scheduled across the year to continue the focus on the selected reading or theme. An author visit may kick off the event, with an on-going lecture series to extend dialogue and discussion. Like an orientation-based program, these common reading initiatives can also be administered by academic affairs, students affairs, or as a collaborative effort.

A *course-based program* is typically located and administered in a particular course or academic department. For example, all students in a first-year seminar course may be required to read a selected book and participate in events and discussions both inside and outside their classes. In this approach, the selected reading may function as a text for the course, reinforcing certain themes such as coming-of-age, multicultural awareness, or technology and human behavior. The reading project is also used to teach and reinforce skills, such as reading and writing.

Community-based programs partner the college or university with the larger community. Many towns and cities are also developing common reading programs, so it is natural to merge the two efforts. If a community or public library reading program already exists, the college or university can invite its students, faculty, and

Campus Case 2.1

Engaging the Campus
Kalamazoo College
Zaide Pixley & Diane Seuss

Kalamazoo College's Summer Common Reading Program was implemented in 1999 by the assistant provost for the first-year experience. The College's initial interest in developing a program arose out of a continued response to the challenge of first-year orientation. As the first day of class can set the timbre for the rest of the course, those first few days with the incoming students can set the tone for their entire four years.

At Kalamazoo, faculty and staff are involved early in the planning process. Once the book selection is announced, volunteers are solicited to lead discussion groups during orientation, and the discussion leaders are one of the first campus groups to meet with the visiting author.

The energy created during orientation reverberates throughout the first week and does a great deal to shape the incoming students' introduction to the campus. One of the most important contributions to the students' experience is the modeling of intellectual values. Inevitably, many students arrive on campus with a judgment of the book: "I loved" (or, more likely) "I hated this book." The common reading activities ask the students to postpone the initial judgment and to instead read for complexity and understanding. Similarly, the issue of relevancy typically arises with each book. Regarding Richard Ford's *Independence Day*, one student asked: "Why should I care about the inner life of some middle-aged realtor?"

Obviously, a single-week program cannot hope to entirely reeducate students on the subjects of judgment and relevancy, but Kalamazoo College has found that this intensive experience sets a tone that leads directly into the first-year seminar. In the seminars, students are asked to explore the vast middle ground between easy binaries and to engage in critical thinking about texts in a way that brings complexity, rather than over-simplification, to issues and ideas.

The Summer Common Reading Program at Kalamazoo College has developed activities that are crucial to its educational mission and traditions. Beginning with the 2004 Commencement, Kalamazoo instituted the tradition of bringing the graduating class's Summer Common Reading author back to campus. The author receives an honorary doctorate and is asked to deliver a short address to the class. In 2004, Richard Ford addressed the graduates with passion, wit, and grace. This tradition provides a distinctive frame of meaning for the students' four years at the College.

staff to join the community in reading the common book. Students at Capital Community College in Hartford, Connecticut, participate in the "One Book for Greater Hartford," a regional effort organized by the Hartford Public Library and designed to engage the community in a shared experience—the reading of one book (Hartford Public Library, 2005). This is an accessible, affordable, and engaging literary event that encourages broad participation and offers opportunities to gather and discuss issues relevant to their community from the summer through the fall. At Capital Community College, students in the learning communities and in other courses are assigned the book. They discuss the reading in class and are required or encouraged to attend community events. The culminating event for the program is the author-led talk and reception at the Hartford Community Library in the fall.

Requiring the Common Reading

On some campuses, the common reading is a requirement of orientation and students are assigned to discussion groups when they arrive on campus. Other programs incorporate the book into a course, such as a first-year seminar, as a required reading with related assignments. However, most campuses strongly encourage or expect students to read the book as part of their transition to college. At Temple University, entering first-year students are "asked" to read the selected book prior to the start of the fall semester. Frequently asked questions during orientation include "Do I have to read it?" and "Is it required?" It is explained to students that they are strongly encouraged to read the book as part of the new student experience, and that it is the expectation and hope that they will participate in activities around the book. Students are informed that some teachers may opt to incorporate or require the book in their classes, but that there is no university-required assignment for the book, nor is there a penalty for non-participation.

Part of the controversy faced by UNC's summer reading program over its selection of *Approaching the Qur'án: The Early Revelations* was the use of the term "required." The program materials noted that the summer reading program was "required" for new students, but the term "required" was meant loosely (i.e., a strong college education requires exposure to new ideas through activities such as summer reading) by program planners. Because both internal and external groups believed that failure to complete the "required" assignment would be noted on the academic record, the wording was subsequently changed to "expected" (J. Deshotels, personal communication, July 2005).

Conclusion

This chapter has touched briefly on the major components of the common reading experience. While the selected text or texts is clearly the centerpiece, such programs involve much more. Successful programs provide opportunities for students to become acclimated to the academic expectations of the institution and to develop important academic skills. Moreover, the common reading can provide a forum for institutions to explore themes or issues important to their educational missions.

Chapter Three

Creating and Implementing Common Reading Programs

Establishing a common reading program requires going beyond setting goals and selecting a type of program (e.g., orientation-based, curriculum-based) to implement. Like any other campus program, common reading programs are most successful when they are integrated into the mission and infrastructure of the college or university. Individuals looking to create common reading programs need to be cognizant of the institutional culture and find ways to build support for the initiative. In creating and implementing a common reading program, campuses should consider:

- Opportunities to build on or connect with other institutional initiatives (e.g., a new retention initiative, a task force to improve new student orientation, a new residence hall or student activities center, the arrival of new leadership)

- Structures and resources needed to support a program

- Conditions for sustaining and institutionalizing a program

- Strategies for promoting the program on campus

Connecting With Other Initiatives

The goals and purposes of a common reading program may be linked to other initiatives or changes happening in the institution. For example, when developing a program, planners should review the institution's mission and goal statements, strategic planning documents, and speeches given by campus leaders to see how the goals for the common reading program might connect to broader objectives for the institution. Planners should also meet with senior academic and student affairs leadership to get a sense of how a common reading program might help meet their units' objectives. Meeting with deans and department heads is also important to gain a sense of their willingness to participate in creating the program, selecting a book, and in sponsoring program events.

First-year experience programs, orientation offices, libraries, or standing faculty committees are all places where the idea of a common reading program may take root. Most common reading programs involve faculty from the beginning, and some campuses begin their reading initiatives as an outgrowth of an existing academic program such as general education, developmental education, learning communities, honors programs, or first-year seminars.

Temple University implemented learning communities in 1993 and a first-year seminar in 1995. When program leadership and faculty talked about ways to enhance feelings of community and learning experiences among students in learning communities, the idea of a common reading program was well received. The common reading program was developed to "provide a common intellectual experience for entering students; bring students, faculty, and members of the Temple community together for discussion and debate; and promote cross-disciplinary thinking and dialogue in learning communities, freshman seminars, and other first-year courses where the text might be discussed" (Temple University, 2005).

The common reading program at Appalachian State University has been in place since 1997. Initial conversations about a reading program began at a 1996 retreat where faculty discussed ways to improve the campus' academic climate. For example, an enduring characteristic of Appalachian's tradition and reputation is its "family climate" (N. Spann & D. Graham, personal communication, August 2004). Yet, faculty worried that growing enrollments would result in the loss of this family feel. Campus Case 3.1 describes how Appalachian State began its program in response to these changes.

Identifying Structures and Resources

Creating a common reading program requires working within existing structures as well as creating new ones. Whether the impetus for a common reading program comes from faculty or administration, academic affairs or student affairs, general questions need to be answered: Who needs to be involved? What are the sources of support or resistance? What will the process be? What resources are available?

Campus Case 3.1

Getting Started

Appalachian State University

Nancy G. Spann & Donnelle Graham

The Summer Reading Program at Appalachian State University began in 1997, but discussions about such a program began a year earlier at a faculty retreat where faculty members discussed the need to enhance the academic climate on campus. Faculty believed the social aspect of college life (i.e., out-of-class activities) was very effective, but that the University needed to put more emphasis on the academic purposes of a college education and to focus on the entering student.

At the beginning, the chairperson of the Mathematical Sciences Department and the director of General Studies collaborated to develop a Summer Reading Program and began to generate interest in the proposal by sharing the vision at various meetings. They sought to involve as many people across campus as possible in the development and implementation of the program. The start-up phase of the program went very smoothly. The coordinators/directors developed a blueprint for the program and presented it to the chancellor, the vice-chancellor for academic affairs, the Administrative Cabinet, the Deans' Council, the Council of Chairs, the Core Curriculum Council, the Academic Policies and Procedures Committee, the Faculty Senate, the Student Development Council, and department chairs in each of the five colleges. Response to and support for the program was overwhelmingly positive.

During the early years, these two individuals coordinated the program with a committee of colleagues representing the various colleges and administrative offices that would have an obvious impact on the successful implementation of the program. The coordination of the Summer Reading Program has changed slightly since its inception, but it continues to be jointly coordinated by a faculty member and a member of the General Studies staff. The program continues to be housed in the Office of General Studies and shares its resources including secretarial staff, a graduate assistant, and administrative oversight. Funding for printing materials and other budget items is provided through student orientation fees. Funding for the author or subject of the book to visit campus and speak at convocation is provided through the University's convocation budget.

One of the defining characteristics of the program is the strong support it receives from the chancellor, senior administrators, and faculty. The Summer Reading Program at Appalachian State is a campus-wide program, and everyone—from food service personnel to senior administrators—is invited to participate as book discussion leaders. The program has brought the University together as a true community and has received such strong support through the years that it has become an integral part of the campus culture.

Identifying Key Constituents

A guiding principle in developing programs is to be as inclusive as possible, as early as possible (Shapiro & Levine, 1999). Most programs are a collaborative effort, and the planning groups typically represent a wide range of constituents, including faculty, student affairs administrators (e.g., vice presidents, associate or assistant vice presidents, deans of students); academic administrators; (e.g., provosts, associate or assistant vice provosts, deans, department chairs); first-year experience staff; librarians; orientation, student activities, and residence life professionals; academic advisors; and students. Whenever possible, the planning process should be open to all who want to be involved. A planning committee need not be large, but work groups may need to be established to focus on specific aspects of the program such as planning events, leading discussions, hosting a visiting author, or assessing the program.

Involving key campus constituents in program planning is vital to the success of the common reading experience. If the initiative includes faculty-led discussion sessions, planners need to determine the ideal size for a discussion session and then calculate how many faculty volunteers are needed to lead the groups. Academic advisors, orientation staff, and others who will be involved in notifying students of the project need to be informed and regularly updated. Individuals, whose venues or offices will sponsor events, also need to be included in the planning.

Organizational culture should always be considered in developing the program. If the program is primarily the responsibility of student affairs, what challenges will the program face in trying to involve faculty? If the program is directed by academic affairs, what do planners need to know and consider about the nature of student participation in campus activities? When the common reading program is a student affairs initiative, planners should reach out to faculty and academic administration, particularly if the goals for the project are to set an academic tone for students arriving on campus. Planners should work with deans and department chairs who have experience bringing speakers to campus to arrange guest lectures. If the program includes faculty discussion leaders, faculty volunteers should be asked their advice on the ideal settings and structures for promoting conversations about a book. If the common reading program is an academic affairs initiative, planners should invite student affairs to partner in the planning of events. Student affairs professionals are the on-campus experts when it comes to activities. Moreover, residence life units have a network of resident directors and resident assistants who can help promote events and encourage groups of students to attend.

Because organizational culture and context is critical to the success of a program, the planning process should be inclusive. The earliest discussions of a common reading program should include conversations with various constituencies about the needs of the campus, the purpose for implementing a common reading program, and ways to build support and involvement for the effort.

The UNC summer reading program is coordinated by the Office of New Student Programs; however, a current strength of the program is its inclusive planning structure. A book selection committee of nine faculty, students, and staff select the reading. A resource group comprised of faculty experts in areas related to the main themes for the selected reading then develop supporting materials, including web resources and events. For example, faculty from the Peace, War, and Defense Curriculum and staff from the ROTC program participated in the resource group for the 2004 selection, *Absolutely American: Four Years at West Point*—a book following a future generation of army officers. A third group, coordinated by the Center for Teaching and Learning, planned and provided training for discussion group facilitators. The Office of New Student Programs worked with all three groups (J. Deshotels, personal communication, November 2004).

Program planners should be prepared to address concerns or sources of resistance. Because buy-in and campus support for the program can help project leaders overcome challenges, the program should avoid being overly associated with one person or office. When there is broad support for an effort, it can be sustained even when one or more early adopters leave the project or institution. Project goals should be clearly defined and aligned with other institutional priorities. There are likely to be other new ideas or programs competing for resources, so a realistic budget should be developed. Partnerships can help spread support and fiscal responsibility for a common reading project across offices so no one unit assumes the financial burden.

Developing a Planning Calendar

A common reading program requires year-round planning. The events for a current selection and assessment of the current initiative typically take place in the fall. Late in the fall and in early winter, campuses typically work on the selection for the upcoming year and begin planning events. However, the planning for the upcoming selection may take place concurrently with events for a current book selection. In the spring, programs typically promote the selected book and upcoming events and prepare for orientation activities. In the summer, new students are introduced to the goals and expectations for the program, faculty participants attend training or information sessions, and marketing continues for planned events. Box 3.1 is a planning calendar for the summer reading program at Temple University.

One of the most important aspects of the planning calendar is the selection of the common reading. It is important that the individuals responsible for the selection have sufficient time to read the books under final consideration. In addition, the selection timetable should be consistent with other planning calendars (e.g., admissions deadlines, orientation schedules, event planning). For example, if the selection is distributed to students as they arrive for orientation in June, the book needs to be selected in enough time to order and receive copies and to prepare resource materials. The selection process is described in greater detail in chapter 4.

Box 3.1

Freshman Summer Reading Project Calendar
Temple University

The planning cycle for the summer reading program begins in mid-fall, shortly after the author visit and the conclusion of events for the current year selection.

September
- Fall events for current selection: author visit, discussion sessions, film series, essay contest, and other activities
- Assessment of current year program begins

October and November
- Fall events for current book continue
- Assessment of current year program continues
- Committee membership invited to return for next year; replacement or additional members invited to join planning committee
- Discussion of book nomination criteria for upcoming year
- Nomination site opened on the summer reading project web site (month of November)

December, January, and February
- Summer reading committee meets to discuss assessment of current year program
- Summer reading committee meets to discuss books nominated by the campus community and to review lists of books other campuses are reading
- Summer reading committee compiles short list of five to seven books for selection of next book
- Committee members read books on short list (winter break)
- Summer reading committee meets to discuss books on short list
- Summer reading committee selects book
- Author or author's representative contacted to determine interest, availability, and costs associated with a campus visit

March, April, and May
- Book selection announced
- Summer reading committee begins planning author visit and related events
- Temple departments contacted and invited to participate in events
- Faculty discussion leaders recruited
- Copies of books ordered for faculty discussion leaders, orientation leaders, resident assistants, new faculty, and other constituents
- Resource materials prepared and ordered, including bookmark to give to new students during orientation
- Web site updated with information on current selection

June, July, and August
- Students informed about Freshman Summer Reading Project during new student orientation
- Discounted book available to students at all on-campus bookstore locations
- Posters distributed to advising centers
- Reminder postcard mailed to students (August)
- Training sessions for faculty discussion leaders
- Fall events confirmed
- Marketing plan for fall events finalized

Funding the Common Reading Program

Discussions about funding should happen early but should not dominate all initial planning conversations. In ideal circumstances, a program would begin with support from multiple campus units; however, it is often the case that support comes from one office or campus leader. When initial funding is secured, it is then important to build coalitions and increase funding for the program and its activities. At Temple, the program was initiated by first-year program leadership in the Office of the Vice Provost for Undergraduate Studies. Initial funds for the author visit and resource materials came from the first-year programs operating budget, with a small contribution from a development fund for student programs. After the success of the first book selection, support and interest in the program grew. Motivated by a desire to be more involved with campus programming, the campus bookstore (managed by Barnes and Noble College Bookstores Incorporated) committed an annual contribution to the project. The Office of Student Activities, a unit within student affairs, committed funds to support the author's keynote address and other related activities, including a film festival. Other academic units help fund essay contest prizes and events such as colloquiums or panel discussions with the author. While planning for the effort is still the primary responsibility of the Undergraduate Studies Office, fiscal responsibility for the program is now shared across campus.

External grants, alumni gifts, or grants from a campus innovation fund are other ways to support activities for the common reading program. In 2004, Bellevue Community College (BCC) in Washington received a National Endowment for the Humanities faculty development grant to develop a faculty seminar to train and support BCC faculty in teaching the selected book.

Developing a Program Budget

Common budget items include copies of books, author honoraria and travel expenses, printing of resource materials, mailings to students, venue rentals, and set-up charges. Author honoraria will vary greatly and are influenced by the popularity of a book or author. The process of negotiating the author's fee may also differ depending on whether a campus contacts an author directly or works through a literary agent. Another significant cost may be the purchase of books to give to students, faculty, or staff. When buying large quantities of a book, the institution may be able to arrange for a volume discount from the publisher or book distributor. If the program does not provide students with a copy of the book, organizers should work with the on-campus bookstore to provide the book to students at a reduced cost or direct students to bargain retailers or lower-priced online book sellers. Box 3.2 is a sample budget for a program that does not provide books to students. Box 3.3 is a budget for a program that provides each entering student with a copy of the book.

Box 3.2

Sample Budget for a Common Reading Program

(Program that does not provide book to students)

Item	Approximate cost
Books for faculty, staff, and select students *Summer Reading Committee, faculty discussion leaders, new faculty, and resident assistants*	$2,000
Author fee	5,000
Author travel and lodging	1,000
Promotional materials - Marketing *Informational posters, banners, bookmarks*	2,100
Reminder mailing to students *Postcard and mailing for approximately 3,500 students*	1,000
Educational materials *Discussion session question guides, essay contest guide, film series flyer*	1,000
Licensing fee for films in film series *Typically ranges from $250 - $1,300 depending on the movie. Older films typically cost less but may sometimes be more difficult to secure.*	800
Essay contest prizes *Dollars awarded to students' on-campus accounts*	400
Event set-up for author book signing and keynote	300
Food *Breakfast with author for reading committee, lunch with students, refreshments at author receptions*	2,000
Promotional materials – Student give-aways *T-shirts (4,000)*	2,000
Miscellaneous expenses	400
Total	**$18,000**

Note. Authors' speaking fees vary greatly. The common reading program on which this sample budget is based has paid author honorariums ranging from $3,000 to $8,000. Other authors contacted by this program, but not engaged for the summer reading program, have sought fees from $10,000 to $15,000.

Box 3.3

Sample Budget for a Common Reading Program

(Program that provides book to students)

Item	Approximate cost
Books for students *Based on an average cost of $12 per book for approximately 300 students.*	$3,600
Books for others (e.g., advisors, faculty)	1,000
Author fee including travel	16,000
Promotional materials - Marketing *Informational posters, banners, bookmarks*	200
Mailings to students *Postcard and mailing for approximately 3,500 students*	600
Educational materials *Discussion session question guides, essay contest guide, film series flyer*	2,000
Essay contest prizes *Dollars awarded to students' on-campus accounts*	500
Event set-up for author book signing and keynote *Previously charged for this but common reading program is now considered part of Convocation costs.*	250
Food for various events *Small book discussions, individual events specific classes may host, lunch with the author (students are selected to attend based on an essay)*	1,000
Promotional materials – Student give-aways *T-shirts, buttons*	2,500
Total	**$27,650**

Note. Authors' speaking fees vary greatly. The common reading program on which this sample budget is based has paid author fees ranging from $15,000 to $18,000 including travel.

Expenses related to resource materials will also differ from campus to campus. A relatively low-cost way to provide students and faculty with supplementary materials is to post documents to a program web site. A more costly option is to provide students with resource binders or folders. Decisions about resource materials should be linked to the goals and expectations for the program.

Costs for activities can vary, and again, partnering with other campus units is an effective way to reduce costs. The office of student activities might have a budget for bringing speakers to campus and may co-sponsor an author visit. If the selected book deals with environmental issues, science or social science departments might be invited to sponsor a breakfast and discussion with the author. If small group discussion sessions will be held in the residence halls, campus dining services might provide meal coupons for faculty discussion leaders.

Checklists for each event can help ensure individuals planning the events have the necessary resources. For example, when planning for an author visit, planners secure funds for the author's fee but must also consider costs associated with the venue (e.g., chair rental, audio visual, room set-up) where the event will take place.

Institutionalizing a Program

When implementing a new program, initial levels of energy and support will promote early success. A "great read" will get the campus energized and involve students in discussions and events. The success of a program, however, should not rest solely on the draw of the book or the goodwill of early planners. Some books will generate more buzz and higher levels of interest than others, so it is important to have a solid infrastructure in place that supports the common reading program across all book selections.

For a program to succeed, an ongoing commitment to the goals and needs of a program is essential. Reading the book, participating in activities, providing resources for events, publicly discussing the project's goals and expectations for participation are all ways that members of the college or university community can show their dedication and investment in the success of the common reading program. Senior campus leadership needs to demonstrate support for the effort continuously and publicly. As discussed earlier, identifying support and building campus-wide buy-in is central to the long-term success of the initiative.

Gardner, Upcraft, and Barefoot (2005) note the critical role that faculty play in first-year student success, but institutions must provide support for faculty involved in first-year initiatives. For example, training sessions for discussion leaders should be scheduled, and teachers who have successfully incorporated a common reading selection in their classes should be invited to share their ideas with others. Planners should also recognize and reward faculty for their participation. If a common reading program is considered important to institutional goals and objectives, faculty participation should be recognized in ways consistent with college or university practices for merit, promotion, or tenure decisions.

Promoting Campus Events

Decisions about promoting campus events should be made alongside decisions about the types of events to hold, because marketing and promotion can be a significant portion of project funds. When developing a marketing plan, program coordinators should consider the goals for the project, determine which promotional activities can best accomplish these goals, and dedicate marketing resources to those activities that contribute to program objectives. For example, if students receive the book during new student orientation, the program should include promotional materials with the book that will remind students of the project goals and expectations for participation. Bookmarks and resource folders can include important information about the book and serve as visual reminders that students are expected to read the book by a certain time.

Many common reading programs are designed to create community. Promotional items such as mugs, magnets, or T-shirts are visual reminders that members of the campus community are engaged in a common activity. These items can be printed with the name of the project or the selected book for the year and may even contain information about upcoming events. In fall 2004, the Freshman Summer Reading Project at Temple gave out free T-shirts, packaged as a book, to faculty discussion leaders, committee members, and the first 200 students to attend the author's talk. When students wear the shirts across campus, the project is promoted and people are reminded of the book for the class of 2004.

Modes and Timing of Communication

Technology allows for lower cost ways to promote events quickly and efficiently. For some, however, more traditional modes of communication remain effective. Posters and flyers should be placed across campus and in locations that students frequently visit. Common reading programs, by nature, promote interaction and face-to-face communication, so a personal touch should be used in promoting programs. The president, provost, vice president for student affairs, student government president, or other campus leaders can send students a letter inviting them to read the common reading selection, the same book they, too, intend to read. If the program is for entering students, faculty members or student mentors should encourage students to read the book and participate in activities.

Listservs and e-mails are an effective way to send reminders and event announcements. Temple's summer reading program relies on its "New Owls Listserv" to remind students of the author's visit and related common reading events. The daily "Temple Announce" e-mail sent to the entire campus community includes regular reminders of the films being shown as part of the summer reading project film series.

If students are first notified in June that they need to read a book before arriving for the start of classes, chances are many of those students will need a reminder in August. While marketing events early allows people to plan and manage their calendars more effectively, the decision to participate is more often a last-minute one. Planners should send frequent reminders, particularly close to the event time. Announcements can also be made at other campus events. Mailings about orientation or new student convocations should include reminders to read the selected book and to attend the sponsored events. Posters or flyers should be displayed in heavily trafficked areas such as the student center, campus bookstore, dining locations, or other areas where students gather regularly. If the program plans to have people handing out flyers, information should be distributed at times when the campus is busy—between classes, during meal times, at bus or train stations at the beginning or end of the day. A schedule of events should be published in regularly disseminated campus publications or calendars. Division heads, deans, department chairs, and other senior administrators should be asked to make announcements at staff meetings. To help promote its summer reading project, the Temple book selection committee considers marketing from the onset. Campus Case 3.2 describes how Temple promotes and markets its reading selection and related activities.

Resources for Program Planners

More and more campuses are implementing common reading programs. As they do, their experiences become general information other campuses can draw on as they implement reading initiatives. Appalachian State maintains a summer reading listserv (summerreading@listproc.appstate.edu) that is a useful resource for communicating with others involved with common reading programs. The list is often used to exchange ideas about selecting books, planning events, and assessing programs. Instructions for subscribing to the list can be found on the web site of the National Resource Center for The First-Year Experience and Students in Transition (http://www.sc.edu/fye/resources/fyr/reading/read02.html). The National Resource Center also maintains a section on its web site devoted to reading programs. Under "first-year resources," there are links to a database of programs and selected readings.

College-based web sites of common reading programs are also a valuable source of information. Many common reading web sites list program goals, describe the book selection process, and list upcoming events. Many also list past selections. Common reading programs vary from campus to campus, and variables such as institutional type and size influence the nature and scope of a program. The experiences of other campuses can be very informative in planning a common reading program; but to take root, a common reading program needs to be consistent with the student, faculty, and organizational context of each campus.

Promoting Common Reading Events
Temple University
Kristen diNovi

Planning and promotion are important components of the Freshman Summer Reading Project at Temple University. The Freshman Summer Reading Committee includes at least one staff member from the Offices of Publications, and News and Media Relations. The committee also includes representatives from Student Activities and Residence Life, two offices that co-sponsor common reading events.

Incoming first-year students are the target audience for promotion of the summer reading project and new student orientation is the primary point at which students are notified about the Freshman Summer Reading Project. During their orientation visit, students receive a bookmark announcing the current selection. The bookmark, designed by the Office of Publications, also informs students that they are expected to read the book and that they can purchase it at a discount at all on-campus bookstore locations.

Another key marketing piece is the summer reading poster, also designed by the Office of Publications. The poster includes more comprehensive information about the selection and dates, times, and locations for the author's visit and other common reading events. Since advising and registration are key components of orientation, all campus advising locations receive copies of the summer reading poster to display in academic advisors' offices and waiting areas. Posters are also displayed in other busy locations such as campus dining centers and residence hall lobbies.

Another print piece is a reminder postcard mailed to all incoming first-year students about three weeks prior to the start of the fall semester. The postcard explains the nature of the project and reminds students to read the book before returning to campus. The postcard also announces the schedule for the author's visit.

Promotion and marketing are a part of the program budget, but as a cost-saving measure, the project places information about the reading selection in existing publications. For example, in 2004 the Freshman Summer Reading Project began including a paragraph about the book and upcoming events in the "move-in guide" published by the Office of University Housing. In 2004, the program partnered with Student Activities to hold a *Caucasia* (2004 common reading selection) Film Series. The films were advertised on the Main Campus Program Board movie posters, on all common reading project print materials, and announcements were posted on the student activities information kiosks. Reminder messages about all common reading events were also sent to students via a new student listserv.

The Office of News and Media Relations assists with internal and external publicity. A story about the project appears annually in both the student-run newspaper and the general campus paper. Announcements of events are sent out regularly through "Temple Today," daily e-mails sent to all members of the campus community. Press kits, including information about the project and various resource materials, are sent to local print and broadcast media. When requested, on-campus or local media are scheduled time with the visiting author for brief interviews.

The Freshman Summer Reading Project web site (www.temple.edu/summerreading) is the central information site for the project and another promotion tool. It states the goals of the program, provides resources for faculty and students, lists the schedule of events for the current selection, and provides information about past selections.

Conclusion

The goals and purposes for the common reading program need to be at the center of planning conversations. Planners should build a program based on common goals, such as creating community and deepening engagement. To build this type of reading community, the planning process should be collaborative. Successful common reading programs are often the shared responsibility of academic affairs, student affairs, and other units on campus. Those involved with building the program should be open and inclusive in the planning and decision-making process. Planners need to identify the structures and resources necessary to implement and sustain a program. The first book selections will likely create an early excitement for the program. The real work comes with using that energy to transform a common reading program into a campus tradition.

Chapter Four

Selecting the Common Reading

A defining activity for common reading programs is the annual selection of the book or readings. Selecting the book is typically the responsibility of a committee that consists of faculty, staff, and students. In some instances, a standing committee, such as a general education committee, might make the choice. On other campuses, the choice may be made by an individual such as a dean of students, associate provost, or first-year experience coordinator. Components of the selection process are interrelated and include who will choose the book, the selection itself, and how the book or reading will be announced.

Responsibility for the Selection

When using a committee approach, it is important that membership be diverse and representative of important constituent groups across campus, including faculty, staff, and students. At Appalachian State University, the committee consists of 15 to 18 individuals representing a variety of offices, several of which work with first-year students: General Studies (i.e., orientation and academic advising), Freshman Seminar, Student Development, Library, News Bureau, Visiting Writers' Series, Faculty Development Center, and Cultural Affairs. A committee of three faculty, three staff, and three students selects the book for the Carolina Summer Reading Program at the University of North Carolina (UNC) at Chapel Hill. A faculty member chairs the group. Committee members serve two-year terms, and a portion of the committee changes annually.

Temple University uses a similar approach when staffing its Summer Reading Committee and aims to include all individuals who will be involved with the planning and marketing of common reading events. Faculty members represent different schools and colleges, and there is almost always at least one representative from the English Department who can discuss readability and the appropriateness of the selection for first-year college students. Offices involved in planning the events and resource materials—Publications, Student Activities, Housing, and News and Media Relations—also participate. A librarian, who directs the library's book club, serves on the summer reading committee as well. Typically, two to three students are in the group, including a second-semester first-year student who recently participated in the common reading. The committee meets throughout the year and is involved in all project activities from selecting the book to planning activities to facilitating discussion sessions and assessing the current year initiative.

Not all campuses use a committee process to select the book. Until 2005, the University of South Carolina's associate provost and dean of undergraduate affairs selected the reading for the First-Year Reading Experience, which was typically a classic of modern American literature. The associate provost then recommended the book to the planning committee. If the title had not been widely read, members of the committee read it and provided feedback. If there were no strong objections to the selection, the book was then announced. In 2005, however, after the associate provost who initiated the First-Year Reading Experience retired, a new associate provost moved toward a committee-directed book selection process and more contemporary selections.

Prior to 2005, the staff of the First-Year Experience (FYE) Program at Gallaudet University selected the book, but members of the campus community—especially reference librarians—were asked for suggestions. FYE leadership also used listservs and networked at annual conferences to solicit recommendations from colleagues at other universities. In 2005, Gallaudet changed their process and moved to a committee approach to generate greater campus-wide ownership for the book and create a greater sense of "common" reading for the entire University community. Faculty, staff, and students now sit on the committee to select the book. In addition, by involving people from across campus, the program was able to promote other first-year experience initiatives.

Selection Criteria

One of the first tasks of a common reading committee is the discussion of the selection criteria. Many of the programs discussed in the monograph use similar selection criteria, slightly modifying the parameters to fit their program goals and campus cultures. Predetermined selection criteria help a committee or campus narrow its choices. Box 4.1 lists some common selection criteria.

Box 4.1

Criteria for Common Reading Selections

- Readability and potential for engaging students
- Literary quality
- Relevance to first-year students, current society, or local community
- Appeal to a wide range of students
- Possibilities for additional programming, especially inclusion in first-year courses or other areas of the curriculum
- Interdisciplinarity
- Richness of content/themes
- Cost (paperback versus hardcover)
- Length
- Likelihood students will have read the book in high school
- Connection to one or more college initiatives or institutional mission
- Accurate and respectful portrayals of diverse cultures
- Potential to spark passionate discussion
- Opportunities for multimedia approaches and creative assignments

Note. Selection criteria are derived from the common reading programs at Bowling Green State University and Bellevue Community College among others.

For colleges or universities interested in bringing an author to campus, the availability of the author might be an additional criterion. If a common reading program features classics, the selection group might consider the availability of an on- or off-campus scholar on the author or book. In the past, the common reading program at University of South Carolina focused on literary classics, aiming to select a stimulating novel of literary quality. An additional consideration was important literary milestones. In 1996, 1997, and 1999 books were chosen to celebrate the 100th birthdays of F. Scott Fitzgerald (*The Great Gatsby*), William Faulkner (*The Bear*), and Ernest Hemingway (*The Sun Also Rises*), respectively.

The selection committee for the Bellevue Community College BCC Reads Program takes into account the reading needs of all students. In addition to selecting a book that is of disciplinary interest across several subject areas, the committee of about 12 people tries to select a book that has an audio version available so that students with visual impairments or learning disabilities can also participate. If an audio version is not available, the program will cover the costs of producing an audio copy of the book.

A value often expressed by those involved with common reading projects is that the text should touch students personally. When the University of Pennsylvania Penn Reading Project selected Mary Wollstonecraft Shelley's *Frankenstein*, remembering that Shelley wrote the novel when she was 18 swayed the committee. Moreover, the view of science presented in the novel, and in the depictions of Frankenstein's monster in countless cinematic adaptations, highlights a number of key issues including the role of scientific inquiry in society, the ethics of science, and the validity of the perception of the "mad scientist" in the popular imagination. So from the vantage point of the committee, the selection had the breadth of appeal likely to compel significant interest. However, the program heard from a number of students that the style of the book—with its epistolary frame narration and extensive dialogue—was challenging. Thus, accessibility and readability are also important considerations.

LaGuardia Community College promotes itself as "the world's community college" and considers the diverse needs of its students when outlining the selection criteria for its reading program. The common reading book is selected by a committee of faculty volunteers, most of whom come from the departments of English as a second language, English, math, humanities, and communication skills. The committee considers how the book can be taught and looks for books that present a range of learning opportunities. Because of its diverse student body, LaGuardia considers some unique selection criteria including "what the book says about American culture and how this book will inform a largely immigrant student body about issues in American culture" (J. E. Clark, personal communication, February 2005).

Many programs consider whether the book is consistent with goals for the program, curriculum, or institutional mission. At Saint Francis University in Pennsylvania, a volunteer committee of faculty, students, and community members, called the Reader's Forum, reads books suggested for the summer reading initiative and forwards a short list of recommendations to the General Education Committee, which is responsible for the final selection. Selection criteria are similar to that of other institutions, but the Saint Francis selection criteria is also closely aligned with its mission. The selected book should be consistent with the Eight Goals of Franciscan Higher Education: (a) a humble and generous attitude toward learning, (b) reverence for all life and for the goodness of all humanity, (c) a global vision, (d) service to the poor and needy, (e) respect for the uniqueness of individual persons, (f) a community of faith and prayer, (g) the spirit of simplicity and joy, and (h) Franciscan presence (Saint Francis University, n.d.). The selected reading should also be consistent with the goals of their General Education Program, which focus on values, skills, and knowledge and should be suitable for inclusion in first-year seminars or as the basis of writing assignments in first-year English. Past selections include Paulo Coelho's *The Alchemist* (the magical story of Santiago, an Andalusian shepherd boy who yearns to travel in search of unimagined worldly treasure) and Jacques Roumain's *Masters of the Dew* (a Haitian novel that describes one man's struggle to keep his little community from starvation during a drought).

Kalamazoo College takes a similar approach to selecting a common reading by paying attention to its general education goals. Because 80 to 85% of the student body studies abroad in the junior year, the College tries to select a common reading that has a multicultural dimension. They also look for books that include the notion of boundary crossing. "What we intend to model for the students is that the life of the mind (and body and soul) crosses disciplinary divides and that this is the heart (body and soul and mind) of the liberal arts enterprise" (Z. Pixley, personal communication, August 2004). A past selection was Ann Patchett's *Bel Canto*, a novel set against the backdrop of South American politics. In the novel, unexpected bonds are forged between terrorists and hostages when people from different countries and continents become compatriots.

The Selection Process

A seemingly endless list of books from which to select a common reading exists. As one member of the Temple Summer Reading Committee asked, "Is our selection pool any book that has ever been written?" To narrow choices, many campuses work from existing lists of titles including national best seller lists, best seller lists from online retailers, book club selections, *The Chronicle of Higher Education*'s regular survey of "What They're Reading on College Campuses," and past selections from other institutions.

At other institutions, planning groups solicit suggestions from the campus community. For example, at UNC-Chapel Hill, book suggestions come from the University community via a campus-wide e-mail, postings to the reading program web site, and recommendations from alumni and the general public submitted via the Chancellor's Office. For the 2005 selection, 224 people offered suggestions about books, and the nominations represented diverse topics and viewpoints. Further, as described in the press release announcing the 2005 book, the selection committee meetings are open. According to senior administration, "an open process helps the campus community and the public better understand the care and thoughtfulness that goes into the choice" (UNC News Service, 2005). The committee discusses the nominations and then selects two to three books, in rank order. The alternate choices are considered only if there are insufficient copies of the first choice in print to meet the program's needs.

Narrowing the possible choices can be a daunting task. The Freshman Summer Reading Committee at Temple goes through several steps to narrow a list of 300 books to a "short list" of five to eight books. The committee solicits nominations in two ways. Students participating in the current year reading project are invited to suggest books when they complete the end-of-project online survey. Faculty and other members of the campus community are invited to nominate books via the project web site. The committee receives spreadsheets that include the book title, author, publication year, and length. Table 4.1 is a sample of books nominated for the 2005 reading selection.

Table 4.1
Sample Listing of Titles Nominated for the 2005 Freshman Summer Reading Selection, Temple University

Title	Author	Year Published	Pages
1984	Orwell, George	1949	336
Angela's Ashes	McCourt, Frank	1996	368
Angels and Demons	Brown, Dan	2001	608
Animal Farm	Orwell, George	1946	144
Beloved	Morrison, Toni	1987	275
Cry, The Beloved Country	Paton, Alan	1948	320
Bluest Eye, The	Morrison, Toni	1965	224
Catcher in the Rye, The	Salinger, J. D.	1951	224
Choke	Palahniuk, Chuck	2001	304
Chosen, The	Potok, Chaim	1967	271
Cider House Rules, The	Irving, John	1999	598
Civil Action, A	Harr, Jonathan	1996	512
Clockwork Orange, A	Burgess, Anthony	1963	192
Coldest Winter Ever, The	Sister Souljah	1999	432
Color of Water, The**	McBride, James	1996	336
Color Purple, The	Walker, Alice	1983	300
Curious Incident of the Dog in the Night-Time*	Haddon, Mark	2003	240
Da Vinci Code, The	Brown, Dan	2003	464
Fear and Loathing in Las Vegas	Thompson, Hunter	1971	204
Fight Club	Palahniuk, Chuck	1996	199
Giver, The	Lowry, Lois	1993	208
Go Ask Alice	Anonymous	1994	159
Invisible Man	Ellison, Ralph	1952	581
Ishmael: A Novel	Quinn, Daniel	1992	263
Johnny Got His Gun	Trumbo, Dalton	1939	243
Joy Luck Club, The	Tan, Amy	1989	352
Lesson Before Dying, A	Gaines, Ernest	1993	272

Continued on next page.

Table 4.1 continued
Sample Listing of Titles Nominated for the 2005 Freshman Summer Reading Selection, Temple University

Title	Author	Year Published	Pages
Life of Pi	Martel, Yann	2002	336
Love in the Time of Cholera	Marquez, Gabriel Garcia	1988	348
Lovely Bones	Sebold, Alice	2002	352
Makes Me Wanna Holler	McCall, Nathan	1994	416
Namesake, The	Lahiri, Jhumpa	2003	291
Native Son	Wright, Richard	1940	432
Nickel and Dimed	Ehrenreich, Barbara	2001	240
Night	Wiesel, Elie	1960	109
*On the Road**	Kerouac, Jack	1957	307
Perks of Being a Wallflower, The	Chbosky, Stephen	1999	213
Things Fall Apart	Achebe, Chinua	1959	272
Things They Carried, The	O'Brien, Tim	1990	416
Tuesdays With Morrie	Albom, Mitch	1997	192

Note. All titles were nominated more than once and came from student surveys, from a university-wide nomination web site (*), or from both sources (**).

The committee reviews the nominations against the selection criteria, eliminating any books not available in paperback or considered too long (400+ pages) for a summer reading. The committee also removes books that might be required reading in first- or second-year Temple courses or anything that a large number of entering students may have read in high school. Other steps in the selection process include reviewing summaries on publisher or bookseller web sites to learn more about the titles remaining on the list and engaging in a discussion of current events or issues of importance to students (e.g., coming-of-age, wellness, diversity). Committee members then read the five to eight books on the short list over the winter break. The committee reconvenes at the start of the spring semester to discuss what they read and to make the final selection.

Over time, committees may establish patterns in their choices. Through the trial and error of past selections, Elon University realized that a key element for their earlier choices had been "authors who are in some ways role models for our students" (S. Braye, personal communication, 2004). When reading *There Are No Children Here* by Alex Kotlowitz, the committee realized that books written in the first-person by authors who can talk directly to students' lives or experiences provide a more powerful experience for students. "Kotlowitz exposed private school students in North Carolina to a world they barely knew, urban kids in Chicago, and helped them understand their responsibilities to the world beyond them, another major goal of the new general studies program" (S. Braye, personal communication, 2004). Campus Case 4.1 describes the two-year process Elon uses to select its common reading text.

When narrowing the choices, those responsible for the selection should be careful to ensure all books under consideration meet the selection criteria and that the book is consistent with the project goals. If copies of the book will be provided to students, an important first step is contacting the publisher to make sure the number of copies needed is available. If an author's visit is the featured event for the program, planners should confirm that the author can visit campus on the desired dates and that the costs associated with the author's visit are within the project budget. At Appalachian State, the co-directors of the Summer Reading Program make general inquiries to the author or author's representatives for all the books under consideration to determine cost and availability and provide this information to the committee.

Announcing the Choice

Once a common reading program is established, a general curiosity develops on campus about which book will be selected each year. There are different ways to announce the selection. Planners or the reading selection committee may post the selection to a campus web site or send an e-mail across campus announcing the book and thanking those who participated in the selection process. The selection may also be covered in student and faculty news publications. If the author's visit is confirmed, all publicity should announce the date(s) of the visit at the same time the book selection is announced.

No book will be universally embraced by the campus community. Some selections will be more popular than others, and some selections may attract controversy. The reaction to the selection can provide valuable teaching moments for students. When a choice is controversial, there are opportunities to discuss important issues such as academic freedom, free speech, and censorship. When there is a strong negative reaction to a choice, it is important that those responsible for the selection not only share the reasons behind the choice but also listen and consider opposing viewpoints. The initial reaction to a choice can form the basis for debates or

Campus Case 4.1

Selecting the Book
Elon University
Stephen Braye

The complex process of selecting a common reading must be completed in a timely manner. At Elon University, the selection process starts in the fall, two years prior to the year in which the selected text will be used. A Common Reading Committee—chaired by a faculty member, with representatives from the faculty, staff, student life, and the student body—solicits suggestions from all areas of the university and reviews books during the fall and spring of that first year. By the end of the spring, the committee narrows the list to approximately six books. All the books must be in paperback and must be reasonably priced. Additionally, the book must:

- Raise interesting issues for discussion in a variety of courses
- Offer an example of good writing
- Be written by a living author available to speak on campus
- Offer incoming students an enjoyable reading challenge
- Address global issues in a challenging manner

During the summer, the committee receives copies of the books to read and shares their reaction with other committee members. As early as possible in the fall semester, the committee makes its decision. Early identification of the book allows time for the university to publicize the book with its incoming first-year students, while allowing the Cultural Programs staff time to schedule a campus talk with the author. It also enables Admissions staff to refer to the book while on the road recruiting and allows the Common Reading Program to be promoted during spring orientation events.

Since 1992 with its first selection of *Thief of Time,* the committee has tried to serve as many parts of the institution as it can by varying the subject or discipline of the text chosen. The committee has attempted to broaden students' perspectives by choosing non-Western authors (Achebe was the first, followed by many more), to speak more directly to the hard sciences by choosing Plotkin and Gould, and even capitalized upon the powerful impact of one selection by using it for two consecutive years.

Elon University Common Reading Selections		
2004	*Nickel and Dimed*	Barbara Ehrenreich
2003	*Falling Leaves*	Adeline Yen Mah
2002	*The Color of Water*	James McBride
2001	*Zenzele*	J. Nozipo Maraire
2000	*Zenzele*	J. Nozipo Maraire
1999	*Questioning the Millennium*	Stephen Jay Gould
1998	*Snakes and Ladders*	Gita Mehta
1997	*Tales of a Shaman's Apprentice*	Mark Plotkin
1996	*Things Fall Apart*	Chinua Achebe
1995	*Ishmael*	Daniel Quinn
1994	*The Measure of Our Success*	Marion Wright Edelman
1993	*There Are No Children Here*	Alex Kotlowitz
1992	*A Thief of Time*	Tony Hillerman

panel discussions that take place when students arrive on campus and have read the book.

One of the more well-documented cases of significant negative reaction to a reading selection is the experience of the Carolina Summer Reading Program at UNC-Chapel Hill. In 2002, the selection committee chose *Approaching the Qur'án: The Early Revelations,* which resulted in a legal challenge from those who believed the text would give new students too positive a view of Islam (Rooney, 2003). The question was also raised about whether a religiously oriented text should be "required" at a public institution. There were also concerns about a focus on the Qur'án due to heightened sensitivity so close to the September 11th terrorist attacks. A few feared that students would be "brainwashed" (J. Deshotels, personal communication, July 2005). The chancellor responded to calls to change the book affirming the institution's commitment to academic freedom.

The 2003 Carolina Summer Reading book, *Nickel and Dimed,* also drew criticism. The book was attacked as "another liberal summer reading selection," and some expressed concern that the University was too liberal overall in its teachings. An additional criticism was that this book was lacking in literary quality and, therefore, not the best choice. However, the book selection raised awareness of low wages on Chapel Hill's own campus, and the lowest paid workers on campus protested for fair wages. An unexpected side effect of the choice was that the Chancellor formed a task force to address wage concerns (J. Deshotels, personal communication, July 2005).

BCC Reads at Bellevue Community College in Bellevue, Washington is a three-year old common reading initiative. In year two, BCC Reads selected *On the Rez* by Ian Frazier, an account of the author's visit to the Pine Ridge Indian Reservation in South Dakota. The selection drew concerns from several groups including a student organization, the First Nations Club, which had members who grew up on the reservation and knew the families and events portrayed in the book. The club's concerns were that the book was written by an outsider, who had visited but not lived on the reservation, and that it portrayed members of the community in negative and stereotyped ways. The College's Diversity Caucus also expressed concerns about the selection. Program coordinators worked with these groups, and when the students selected an alternative book, *Lakota Woman,* which First Nations Club members felt was a more sensitive, well-rounded perspective on Native American life told from an insider's perspective (D. Douglas, personal communication, November 2004 and July 2005), BCC Reads supported the selection and also funded events around the alternative book choice.

Such controversies may draw significant attention to reading programs, leading to increased participation from students, faculty, staff, and members of the surrounding community. Level of interest in the program and the announcements of the selected book may also increase. At UNC-Chapel Hill, four television stations filmed the final selection committee meeting at which the 2004 selection, *Absolutely American: Four Years at West Point,* was announced. The homepage of the University's web site included a link to the news release announcing the 2005 selection, *Blood Done Sign My Name* (a book that examines the civil rights struggle in the South by focusing on the murder of a young black man, Henry Marrow, in 1970, a tragedy that dramatically widened the racial gap in the author's hometown of Oxford, NC).

Conclusion

While common reading programs are about more than a book, the book in many ways defines the program. Selecting the book is the critical first step in planning the reading experience. Selected books should be consistent with the college or university mission, the published criteria for selecting the book, and the overall project goals. Committees or individuals responsible for the choice should invite members of the campus community to participate in the selection process by nominating books.

The process for selecting the book and the choice itself will often be the subject of curiosity, even scrutiny. While many will be pleased with the choice, others may be disappointed, disinterested, or even angry. Some titles will be more popular than others, and the selection committee should consider past and recent successes and failures when making future selections. Committees can learn from the experiences of others by using listservs to poll other campuses about their students' reactions to a book or their campus' dealings with a particular author. When the selection process is organized, selection criteria are clearly articulated, and those responsible for making the choice have the support and information they need, the process can be a positive learning experience for all involved.

Chapter Five

Planning Events and Activities for Common Reading Programs

Jodi Levine Laufgraben & Christopher Dennis

Many common reading programs share the goal of creating community by bringing faculty, students, and other campus groups together to share a common experience. The books selected for common reading programs tend to be interdisciplinary in nature or incorporate multiple issues and themes that encourage discussion and debate. This chapter focuses on designing the settings in which community building and intellectual exchanges occur.

Planning Events

The goals for the common reading program, timing of activities, intended audiences, available resources, and responses to previous books and activities should be considered when planning events. For example, if the goal is to create community, campus events need to bring people—particularly students and faculty—together to talk about the reading. If improving reading and writing skills are important goals, the program should be connected to the curriculum. Moreover, students should be given opportunities to write and talk about the book. When multiple goals for a program exist, the planning committee should consider a range of activities.

The timing of activities is also closely aligned with the goals for the program. When common reading programs are components of new student orientation, events are featured during orientation and welcome activities. For example, some programs provide the students with a copy of the book during their initial orientation visit and then organize students into discussion groups when they return to campus for welcome events or the start of the academic term. Other programs identify a theme for the common reading selection and incorporate that theme in activities planned across the fall term or entire academic year.

Common reading programs may be focused on a single audience or on multiple audiences. When the program is aimed at new students, many of the activities are planned for orientation, the opening of the academic year, or inclusion in first-year courses such as college composition or first-year seminars. When a goal of the common reading program is to engage the campus and the larger community in an intellectual exchange, activities need to be planned at multiple times and in multiple settings. Events can then be scheduled at on- and off-campus venues. For example, exhibits or lectures can take place at both the campus library and a community library.

In addition, activities should be attractive to students' diverse backgrounds, interests, and learning styles. Visual learners may find films and performances more appealing, while other students may be drawn to interactive opportunities such as discussion sessions or question and answer periods with an author. Planning both small and large group activities allow the students to interact with peers and faculty. Author's visits or an invited lecture also provide multiple opportunities for engagement around the reading's major themes.

As discussed earlier, planners need to consider available resources. Many programs select books by living authors and invite the author to campus for a one-day or multi-day visit. When an author's visit is not possible, common reading events can be linked to regularly planned campus activities such as a lecture series at which a faculty member presents on a topic related to themes raised in the common reading.

Finally, activities should be planned using knowledge of what does and does not work on an individual campus. If the majority of students commute, activities should be scheduled when students are most likely to be on campus. On residential campuses, programming is more easily spread across the day or held in the evening. Planners should survey students about events they would like to attend and why. They should consult with individuals on campus who regularly plan activities about times and venues that attract large numbers of students. At each planned event, some type of feedback should be collected. At the end of the project, planners should meet to debrief and talk about activities that were successful and what might have been done differently to improve events that were less successful or poorly attended. Information collected should be used to plan for future events.

Types of Events

Program planners should develop consistent activity offerings, but also be creative and let the selected book drive planning decisions. Certain activities, such as an author visit, discussion sessions, and book signings, can become rituals that faculty, staff, and members of the community eagerly anticipate every year. Other activities, such as film series, performances, or exhibits, may be planned around the unique content of a selected book. Box 5.1 lists events typically associated with the common reading program.

Author's Visit

For students, the opportunity to meet an author is an exciting benefit of a common reading program. The author can participate in a variety of activities during a campus visit, but an address to the campus community could serve as the capstone event and is a good opportunity to bring people together. During a question and answer session, the readers can exchange ideas with the author and ask questions about the book, the author's writing process, or the author's next project. The author can have breakfast, lunch, or dinner with smaller groups of students, faculty, or staff. At Otterbein College, the visiting author participates in a progressive dinner featuring different courses at three residence halls. When the project includes a community component, the author can also spend time off campus. At Appalachian State University, the visiting author or speaker holds a book signing and reading at the local public library.

Box 5.1

Events Associated With the Common Reading Experience

- Author's visits
- Book signings
- Discussion sessions with faculty
- Lecture series
- Art exhibits or theatrical performances
- Library exhibits or resources
- Film series
- Essay contests
- Service or volunteer opportunities
- Special events (e.g., ceremonies, field trips)

A schedule might also include opportunities for the author to visit classes. At Elon University, the author is on campus for two or three days and visits Global Experience courses to discuss themes in the book. At Temple, students in one learning community are annually selected to have lunch with the author. The selected community is typically exploring themes related to the book, and the teachers in the community work with students prior to the visit to generate discussion topics and questions.

Danzy Senna, author of the novel *Caucasia*, visited Temple University in fall 2004. The novel is the story of a biracial girl growing up in 1970s Boston, and the story was relevant to issues of race, identity, and crime that students were discussing in their criminal justice and college composition courses. She began her day with a welcome breakfast with members of the summer reading committee and faculty who volunteered to lead discussion sessions. Senna's visit also included a session on creative writing, a book signing, lunch with students in the criminal justice learning community, and a talk to the University community. In addition to the activities listed, her morning schedule was adjusted to include time for an interview with students from the campus television station. Box 5.2 provides the schedule for her visit to Temple.

Box 5.2

Sample Schedule for One-Day Author's Visit
Temple University

Selection: *Caucasia* by Danzy Senna

8:30 a.m.	Author breakfast with members of the summer reading committee and faculty discussion leader volunteers
9:30 a.m.	Discussion on creative writing (sponsored by the Department of English, open to the university community)
11:00 a.m.	Interview with on-campus student television station
11:30 a.m.	Lunch with students enrolled in a social sciences learning community
1:15 p.m.	Book signing for students and members of the campus community
2:30 p.m.	Address to university community followed by a question and answer session
4:00 p.m.	Reception for visiting author (open to all)
5:00 p.m.	Author departs campus

Note. Author arrived on campus evening prior to visit.

In 2004, entering students at Appalachian State read *A Hope in the Unseen* by Ron Suskind. The book chronicles the experience of Cedric Jennings, an inner-city high school student who goes to Brown University. Jennings spent two days at Appalachian State; and during his visit, he spoke at a campus convocation, taped an interview for an on-campus television station, visited with local high school students, attended an event at the community library, had lunch with students in a living/learning center, and participated in a session on surviving college. Box 5.3 provides the schedule for this visit.

Box 5.3

Sample Schedule for a Multi-Day Author's Visit
Appalachian State University

Selection: *A Hope in the Unseen* by Ron Suskind (Campus visitor: Cedric Jennings)

Wednesday, September 1, 2004

	Mr. Jennings arrives

Thursday, September 2, 2004

10:00 a.m.	Convocation
12:00 p.m.	Luncheon at Appalachian House with campus administrators and special guests hosted by Chancellor Kenneth Peacock
1:30-3:45 p.m.	Free time for Cedric Jennings
4:00-5:00 p.m.	"Appalachian Perspective" television interview taping
5:15-6:30 p.m.	Dinner at Broyhill with Cedric Jennings and Summer Reading Committee members
7:00-8:30 p.m.	A visit with local high school students at the Plemmons Student Union hosted by Student Support Services

Friday, September 3, 2004

8:00-9:00 a.m.	Special breakfast with the Summer Reading discussion leaders
10:00-11:30 a.m.	"Meet Cedric Jennings," a community event hosted by the Watauga County Public Library. Coordinated by Janice Pope (Summer Reading Committee) and Evelyn Johnson (Watauga County Public Library)
11:45-1:15 p.m.	Lunch with Watauga College first-year students in the Great Hall at the Living Learning Center
1:30-3:00 p.m.	Survival 101: College & Beyond, for all students, faculty, and staff. Sponsored by IDS, Multicultural Affairs, Watauga College, and Freshman Seminar
3:00 p.m.	Mr. Jennings departs.

When the University of Pennsylvania selected Tom Stoppard's *Arcadia* (a play that moves back and forth between centuries exploring such topics as the nature of truth and time and the difference between the classical and romantic temperaments), the playwright was persuaded to visit campus to give a lecture; meet with faculty in English, mathematics, and physics to discuss fractals and the second law of thermodynamics; and meet with groups of first-year students in a variety of settings, especially Penn's College Houses. Notoriously diffident when it came to visiting campuses to discuss his work, Stoppard agreed to the visit when asked if he would be curious to see in person how a new generation of students experienced his play. The lecture was attended by many theater directors in the Philadelphia area and at least one arranged with Stoppard to put on a production of his play the next year. The mayor's office presented a Liberty Bell replica to Stoppard. Thus, the *Arcadia* reading experience itself gave way to a series of engaging events that rippled out from the campus across the city.

For many programs, the author's visit is the main activity. There are programs, however, that choose not to invite an author to campus, typically due to scheduling, availability, or resource issues. Other activities such as discussion sessions, a lecture by a prominent faculty member, concerts, library exhibits, or theatrical performances can then serve as a featured event.

Book Signing

A book signing is a typical component of an author's visit. Planners should set aside enough time for interested individuals to get their books signed and hold the signing in a space conducive to long lines and crowds. The book signing personalizes the project for students and is an opportunity for members of the campus community to meet the author. The book signing is also an ideal time to get pictures of the author with students to use in future marketing materials or place on the project web site to commemorate the visit. One way to facilitate a book signing is to provide post-it notes or pieces of scrap paper on which individuals waiting in line to get their books signed can write their names. The author then glances at the paper before personalizing and signing the book. This keeps the line moving and helps prevent misspelled names.

Discussion Sessions

Discussion sessions engage students around the themes of the book and are an ideal setting to bring students together with their teachers and peers to discuss what they have read. Discussion sessions can be a required or voluntary component of the common reading program and are often incorporated into orientation activities. To maximize opportunities for interaction and dialogue, students and discussion leaders should be organized into small groups. Discussion sessions are a good opportunity to involve faculty in the common reading program, but discussion leaders can also be student affairs staff, administrators, academic advisors, upperclass students, or other members of the campus community. Program planners should schedule a training or book discussion session for the discussion leaders before the event. At Appalachian State, the faculty development center sponsors workshops throughout the summer. The training is a good opportunity for discussion leaders to talk about the goals for the project, the themes in the book, and strategies for encouraging conversation.

Discussion sessions can be held before or after an author's visit or featured speaker. At Appalachian State, when students arrive on campus for the second phase of orientation, they participate in a discussion facilitated by a faculty volunteer or staff member. Gallaudet University sponsors multiple types of discussion sessions. When the selected book was *Tuesdays With Morrie* (Mitch Albom's chronicle of his visits with his college professor during the elder man's final year of life), the social work department showed the made-for-television movie about the book and hosted a discussion for students, faculty, and staff. The Office of Multicultural Student Programs hosted a book discussion lunch group, and the library held a panel discussion open to the community. At Temple, discussion sessions were designed to attract resident and commuting students. Hour-long discussion sessions called "A Book and A Bite" were held during breakfast, lunch, and dinner times at various campus dining locations. Faculty volunteered to lead the discussions.

Discussion sessions can also be incorporated into regularly scheduled class activities. At Kalamazoo College, students participate in small groups formed by dividing first-year seminar classes into discussion groups. The seminar instructor often leads one of the two groups. One of the tasks for the discussion groups is to generate questions to ask the author during the question and answer colloquium, the concluding event of the author's visit.

Discussion sessions held after the author's talk or a keynote event allow students to continue the dialogue, share their perceptions of the book, and raise additional questions. At the University of South Carolina, students meet in discussion groups immediately following the keynote address. Faculty and staff members lead the discussion groups, and University 101 students typically meet with their instructors (who are usually staff members, but may also be faculty members). During a two-hour block, students discuss the book and visit exhibits organized for the First-Year Reading Experience (C. Linder, personal communication, July 2005).

The Penn Reading Project's principle of organization includes resident advisers, advanced undergraduates, and live-in graduate assistants in the college house system who bring groups of new students in the residence halls together with faculty leading discussion groups. Leveraging the residential organizational structure is useful logistically, because the reading project conveys to groups of students, who will be living together for much of the academic year, some sense of what the institution values as important: reading books; meeting with faculty and peers to discuss ideas; sharing views (even when or especially when they diverge); developing a feel for academic life; and how, as a person new to a community of scholars, one might share in intellectual give and take. The Penn model includes a number of special discussion sections organized for commuting and non-residential, first-year students. For discussions that take place before the start of classes, the experience can give new students a sense of what a college class is and what participating in a discussion on the college level might be like.

Invited Lecture or Lecture Series

A lecture series involves on-campus faculty or visiting speakers from a variety of departments and disciplines in intellectual dialogue around the themes in the selected book. If the selected book is a classic or the author is deceased or unavailable, an invited lecture or lecture series can be the main event for a common reading program. At the University of South Carolina, when the author does not visit, a speaker with expertise on the book, author, or subject matter delivers the keynote address. For example, George Plimpton addressed the first-year class when J. D. Salinger's *Catcher in the Rye* was selected because Plimpton was a popular literary figure and an expert on contemporary literature (C. Linder, personal communication, July 2005).

Exhibits or Theatrical Performances

The events associated with a common reading program should appeal to the diversity of students' learning styles and interests. Exhibits and performances can help students visualize the themes depicted in the reading; learn more about the social, historical, or cultural setting of a text; or express their own creative interpretations of a work. When students at Kalamazoo College read *Bel Canto*, a novel that combines music and dramatic intrigue, sopranos performed arias at the opening of the panel discussions and Colloquium.

The University of Pennsylvania's selection in the first year of its program was Euripides' *Bacchae*—the classical text perhaps most radical in exploring the boundaries of identity, including gender identity, and the limits and intersection of divine and political power. The selection was enriched by a campus production of the Nigerian 1986 Nobel Prize winner Wole Soyinka's translation of the play, *The Bacchae of Euripides: A Communion Rite*. Soyinka was invited to attend the production but was unable to come because of transportation difficulties.

Library Exhibits or Resources

Librarians can provide valuable information on resources related to the common reading program. Library exhibits can feature information about the book, author, subject matter, or a historical period. Exhibits can be located within a campus library, or the resource information can be incorporated into the project web site. The common reading committee at Bowling Green State University is chaired by the first-year experience librarian. In 2004, Bowling Green selected Tim O'Brien's *The Things They Carried*, a book that focuses on the members of a single platoon during the Vietnam War and the things they carried into battle (e.g., M-16s, grenade launchers, candy, Kool-Aid, cigarettes), the things they carried inside, and the nightmares they carried home. To coincide with the selection, the library featured an historical display on the Vietnam War. At Temple, reference librarians prepared a web site that contained background information about the author, book, and its historical context. For the 2005 selection, *West of Kabul, East of New York* (Tamim Ansary's personal account of a life lived in two very different cultures, Islamic Afghanistan and the secular West), the library resource page included a list of library print resources on Afghan history (Temple University Libraries, 2005).

Film Series

Films are an excellent complement to common reading experiences as they help students visualize the issues raised by the reading(s) or in discussions about the book. They can also provide background on the historical or cultural context in which a book is set. For its 2004 selection, *Caucasia*, Temple University showed three films as part of its *Caucasia* Film Series. The films were selected to build on themes raised in the story: (a) the childhood, life, and family dynamics of a young mixed race girl "passing" as white (*Imitation of Life*, Universal, 1959); (b) racial tensions in the 1960s (*Love Field*, Orion, 1992); and (c) racial tensions among inner city youth and the emotional impact of parent-child relationships (*A Bronx Tale*, Savoy, 1993). The film showings were listed on University cinema posters, and a flyer detailing the films and show times were distributed to students attending discussion sessions.

When first-year students at Kalamazoo College read *A Gesture Life* by Chang-Rae Lee, the campus showed Dai Sil Kim-Gibson's documentary "Silence Broken: Korean Comfort Women." The book's main character has a forbidden affair with a Korean comfort woman—a woman taken against her will to provide sexual favors for the men in the battalion—during World War II. The film provided important background information and historical context for the student readers.

Essay or Creative Contests

Essay or creativity contests connect the reading, writing, and critical thinking components of a common reading program. Essay topics are closely aligned with the main themes in the reading, and the topic is typically developed by the committee responsible for selecting the book or by faculty involved in project activities and discussions. Creativity contests invite students to explore the central themes of the book from a variety of perspectives and through the use of different media.

At the University of South Carolina, faculty from the art department coordinate the annual First-Year Reading Experience Poster Contest. Graphic design students are assigned the task of creating a poster depicting the book. One poster is selected as the official poster of the First-Year Reading Experience, but all posters are displayed on campus either in the event check-in area or the University's Visitor Center. The selected poster image is also used to create a postcard mailed to students during the summer to remind them of the event. Students also visit the poster exhibit with their discussion groups.

The BCC Reads program at Bellevue Community College sponsors an annual scholarship contest funded by the Faculty Association and the College's Foundation. Students are encouraged to submit a creative submission depicting the book. The guidelines for the contest are relatively open, and entries represent diverse disciplinary approaches to the book. Entries have included paintings, essays, musical compositions, poetry collections, board games, and web pages. All entries are exhibited. Approximately five winners are chosen each year, and winners receive a one-quarter tuition scholarship. The contest is not only an opportunity for greater student involvement in the reading program but is also a valuable assessment opportunity as the entries are often powerful evidence of how students connect the book to their personal experiences. In spring 2004, there were 55 submissions for the book *On the Rez*.

Writing has always been a component of the reading program at Gallaudet University. Initially, the English Department sponsored an essay contest for students. Winners received a gift and were invited to lunch with the author. In 2004, Gallaudet implemented a new letter writing contest. Students submitted a letter to the First-Year Experience Program describing why they should be chosen to have lunch with the author(s). The director and several faculty members reviewed the letters. In the first year of the letter writing campaign, the program received 30 letters, and 25 students were invited to lunch. As described by the director of the First-Year Experience: "WOW...talk about a powerful experience for me. I am humbled by the backgrounds of some of our students. Lots of good things have happened as a result—students sharing, faculty understanding, and it will become an article for our *Gallaudet Today Magazine*" (C. Andersen, personal communication, October 2004).

Service or Volunteer Opportunities

Some readings may lend themselves to a volunteer or community service activity. Students can further explore themes raised in the book by participating in an on- or off-campus community service initiative. When students at Bellevue Community College read *When the Emperor Was Divine* by Julie Otsuka, they participated in a service-learning project partnering them with members of the community who had been interned during World War II. Students learned about internment from those with first-hand experiences, while helping the members of the community write their memoirs. When Temple selected *Fast Food Nation* as its 2002 summer reading, first-year seminar students were encouraged to volunteer at the Philadelphia Food Bank. Students learned about food supply and distribution in Philadelphia and were able to contribute this knowledge to in-class discussions about the food supply in America.

Special Events

Certain books may lend themselves to special events. When it selected *When the Emperor Was Divine* as the 2004-2005 BCC Reads selection, Bellevue Community College planned a Day of Remembrance connected to the National Day of Remembrance marking the anniversary of the executive order for Japanese American internment. The Bellevue Community College events were free and open to the public and included readings, a keynote address, films, and discussions. When Temple students read *West of Kabul, East of New York,* the Office of Student Activities sponsored a field trip to a local restaurant featuring ethnic cuisine and a presentation on the Afghan American community in Philadelphia.

The University of Pennsylvania's selection of *Arcadia* turned out to be rich in many respects. In 1995, the New York production of *Arcadia*, directed by Trevor Nunn, was being performed at the Lincoln Center Theater at the Beaumont. Four of the actors—Jennifer Dundas, Blair Brown, Robert Sean Leonard, and Victor Garber—visited the campus and offered a "master class" for some theater students, discussing with them how Stoppard had prepared them to dramatize the challenging verbal density and content of the play. They also put on a few sample scenes of the play and discussed with aspiring acting students what a career in theater entails.

Events such as library exhibits, film series, or panel discussions not only feature the book but also invite students to visit various programs and offices that they are likely to use throughout their college careers, such as the library, student activities office, or the campus tutoring center.

Faculty Development

If the expectation is that the common reading selection will be incorporated into classes, the common reading program should provide support and resources for teachers. It is important that all teachers who are asked or invited to incorporate the selected text into their courses or lead discussion groups understand the goals of the common reading project. Information or training sessions are a useful opportunity for faculty to receive resource materials and talk with their colleagues about ways to integrate the common reading into their existing course materials.

Most common reading programs plan small-group discussions around the selected book. The sessions—whether led by faculty, upperclass students, or staff—are important opportunities for individuals to participate in academic conversations about the meaning of a book, the issues it raises, or personal connections to the content. These discussions are teaching and learning moments for all participants. Preparing for these sessions presents a learning opportunity as well. When the Penn Reading Project selected Tom Stoppard's play *Arcadia*, they brought in the undergraduate chair of mathematics to teach the discussion leaders about fractals, visual depictions of iterated algorithms, and the interest in Fermat, whose theorem is present in the play's plot.

At Temple's annual first-year seminar instructor workshop, copies of the common reading selection are provided to all instructors and peer teachers. Beginning in summer 2004, the training workshop included a mock book discussion led by one of the members of the summer reading committee. To prepare faculty members to discuss *Caucasia*, an English professor who teaches courses on race led sessions with the faculty discussion leaders to model conversations about race. The faculty in these two-hour sessions were both teachers and learners, sharing their own personal experiences with race, identity, and family relationships. There was great energy in the room as teachers considered the many ways they might share their experiences with this book with the students they met in September.

At Bellevue Community College, the BCC Reads program sponsors a session—at the regularly scheduled fall faculty development day—on teaching the selected book. Each year, about 50 faculty use the BCC Reads selection in their various classes. In addition to the scheduled training, The Center for Liberal Arts at Bellevue submitted and received a National Endowment for the Humanities (NEH) grant to develop a seminar for faculty around its 2004-2005 common reading selection, *When the Emperor Was Divine*. The seminar was designed to prepare faculty to teach the book, and the grant also provided resources for the campus to sponsor a series of cultural events and speakers across the year. The seminar included texts, speakers, films, and field trips. Box 5.4 is the Faculty Seminar Syllabus. Other resources for faculty include materials that the library puts on reserve, including a reader's guide, to assist teachers and students (D. Douglas, personal communication, November 2004).

Resource Materials

Typically, the common reading program leadership, in collaboration with the reading selection committee or other groups organized to assist in planning the program, is responsible for developing resource materials. These materials help guide students in their reading and understanding of the book and also help faculty members incorporate the book into classroom activities. Developing the resource materials is also another opportunity to invite others to help with planning and create buy-in among faculty and staff. Campus librarians are a particularly valuable resource in compiling such materials.

Box 5.4

Faculty Seminar
Bellevue Community College

1. OVERVIEW AND INTRODUCTION (November)

Texts:

- Japanese American Citizens League National Education Committee. (2002). *A lesson in American history: The Japanese American experience* (4th ed.). San Francisco: JACL National Education Committee.
- Otsuka, J. (2003). *When the emperor was divine*. New York: Anchor.

Field Trip:

- Wing Luke Museum and Panama Hotel

2. HISTORY (December-January)

Texts:

- Daniels, R. (1993). *Prisoners without trial: Japanese Americans in World War II*. New York: Hill and Wang.
- Kashima, T. (2003). *Judgment without trial: Japanese American imprisonment during World War II*. Seattle: University of Washington Press.

Speaker(s):

- Roger Daniels, Charles Phelps Taft Professor of History, University of Cincinnati
- Tetsuden Kashima, professor, Department of American Ethnic Studies, University of Washington

Film(s):

- *Rabbit in the Moon*

3. STORIES OF INTERNMENT (January-February)

Texts:

- Harth, E. (2001) *Last witnesses: Reflection on the wartime internment of Japanese Americans*. New York: Palgrave.
- Inada, L. F. (2000). *Only what we could carry: The Japanese American internment experience*. Berkeley: Heyday Books.

Continued on next page.

Box 5.4 continued

Faculty Seminar
Bellevue Community College

4. THE WASHINGTON STATE EXPERIENCE (February-March)

Texts:

- Dubrow, G., & Graves, D. (2002). *Sento at Sixth and Main.* Seattle: Seattle Arts Commission.
- Brown, G. R. (2002, March/April). Identity and erasure: Roger Shimomura. *Asian Art News.*

Speaker(s):

- Roger Shimomura, former internee and visual artist
- Frank Kitamoto, former internee and president, Bainbridge Island, WA Japanese American Community

Field Trip:

- Bainbridge Island

5. RESISTANCE AND AFTERMATH (March-April)

Texts:

- Okada, J. (1976). *No-no boy.* Seattle: University of Washington Press. (optional)
  Speaker(s):
- Frank Abe, filmmaker *(Conscience and the Constitution)*

Film(s):

- *Conscience and the Constitution*
- *Children of the Camps*
- *Beyond Barbed Wire*

6. MEMORY AND RESPONSIBILITY (April-May)

Speaker(s):

- Anna Tamura, landscape architect, National Park Service and planning coordinator, Minidoka Internment National Monument
- Julie Otsuka, author, *When the Emperor Was Divine*
- Tom Ikeda, executive director, Densho: The Japanese American Legacy Project

Reference Text:

- Report of the Commission on Wartime Relocation and Internment of Civilians (CWRIC). (1997). *Personal justice denied.* Seattle: University of Washington Press.

Program planners or the selection committee can identify themes raised in the book and can then invite relevant and interested faculty to develop supporting materials. For example, if the reading explores race and identity, sociology professors or other social scientists who are disciplinary experts in these areas can be invited to suggest resource ideas. Resource materials might include:

- Guided reading questions

- Supplemental/additional readings

- Information about the author

- Material on the historical context

- Book reviews

- Related web sites

Guided reading questions are intended to help the reader explore and understand the book's main themes and can also be used to facilitate discussions. Members of the common reading selection committee and others involved in the planning of events may be invited to suggest questions. The web sites of other common reading programs that may have recently used the same selection can be useful sources of information. In addition, many publishers' web sites now include guided reading questions and resources for many of their commonly selected book club titles.

Many common reading programs prepare discussion guides for students and the faculty/staff discussion leaders. At LaGuardia Community College, the faculty and staff that serve on the First-Year Experience Committee serve as discussion leaders for the book. Discussions are held at Opening Sessions, a whole campus event welcoming students to the college. The discussion guide includes the schedule for the day, suggestions for organizing the discussion session, an overview of themes in the book, and approaches to discussing the book. The guide also includes a list of helpful resources. Box 5.5 is an example of a discussion guide.

Lists of suggested readings encourage students and other members of the campus community to explore a topic beyond the selected book. Suggested readings might include other works by the author, books on similar topics, or readings about the historical context. Many common reading programs aim to promote reading for pleasure and intellectual discovery. Providing students with a list of related readings can help motivate them to continue reading independent of any required or expected reading assignment. For example, with its 2005 reading selection, *West of Kabul, East of New York,* students in one first-year seminar were asked either to see a film related to themes depicted in the book (the films are part of a film series scheduled as part of the summer reading program) or to read *The Kite Runner,* a work of fiction that explores related issues.

Box 5.5

Faculty Guiding Questions for Discussion Groups at Student Opening Sessions
LaGuardia Community College

The Laramie Project

Organizing Your Session

What makes the faculty-led discussion sessions such a rich experience for students [is] your creativity and the variety of approaches to leading discussion on the common reading. This year is no exception. What follows is a brief list of ideas for leading discussion on the play. Feel free to devise your own session plans. These suggestions simply serve as a possible springboard for your own ideas. Please feel free to borrow liberally or to go in another direction entirely. You may want to begin your session by determining how many students have read the play. Usually, many students have read the common reading in its entirety. Sometimes, groups of students receive the book at Opening Sessions, so you should prepare for a mixed group. Most of all, have a fun and engaging session with the students!

General Themes in The Laramie Project

This year's common reading focuses on many different issues such as homophobia, community, sexual politics, class differences, dialogue, hate crimes, religion, justice, and tolerance versus acceptance.

Approaches to Discussing The Laramie Project

1. Associative Exercises (helpful for groups who have not read the entire play).

Role play/discussion: As *The Laramie Project* is a play, you might choose to have students read certain scenes aloud and discuss them. Suggested scenes: "Moment: Alison and Marge" (pp. 14-17), "Moment: Matthew" (pp. 18-20), "Moment: The Gem City of the Plains" (pp. 46-49), and "Moment: Homecoming" (pp. 62-64).

Intolerance discussion: Try one of two interactive exercises to help students connect homophobia to other forms of intolerance. Here is the first: hang blank banner paper around the room. Provide markers and pens. Invite students to write "hate words" and "slang." Then, as a group, discuss the history and significance of the words. Help students make connections among homophobia, racism, sexism, classism, and ableism.

The second is a variation on this exercise. Obtain photographs of different moments of intolerance in American history. I sometimes create a "gallery" of photographs around the room with images of the Ku Klux Klan, the Japanese American internment camps, signs for "Colored Water Fountains," the Civil Rights movement, child labor, Native Americans (particularly images from reservations), women engaged in "traditional" forms of domestic labor, and the fence from Laramie. I ask students to identify the images and then, as with the exercise above, connect different forms of intolerance and prejudice to homophobia.

Continued on next page.

Box 5.5 continued

Faculty Guiding Questions for Discussion Groups at Student Opening Sessions
LaGuardia Community College

Hate crimes discussion: In the past several years, there have been a number of widely publicized hate crimes. Here in the New York area, you might consider finding articles (available on EBSCO through our library) on hate crimes such as those regarding Sakia Gunn and Jessica Horatio Mercado (you can also find a helpful article online at: http://www.hrc.org/Template.cfm?Section=Home&CONTENTID=10061&TEMPLATE=/Content-Management/ContentDisplay.cfm)

A variation on this exercise would be to connect homophobia and assumptions about people to racism. You might extend the discussion to include police "profiling" in its most extreme cases such as Abner Louima and Amadou Diallo.

Universal human rights discussion: You might ask students to think about hate crimes in the context of the *Universal Declaration of Human Rights.* Provide students with a copy of the declaration and, as a group, use it to talk about homophobia and prejudice.

2. Textual Analysis (useful with groups who have read the play in its entirety)

In his introduction to the play, Kaufman writes, "There are moments in history when a particular event brings the various ideologies and beliefs prevailing in a culture into sharp focus. At these junctures, the event becomes a lightning rod of sorts, attracting and distilling the essence of these philosophies and convictions. By paying careful attention in moments like this to people's words, one is able to hear the way these prevailing ideas affect not only individual lives but also the culture at large" (p. v). As you lead students in discussion, you may want to use this idea as a touchstone for your larger conversation. Given that you will have students of mixed skill levels in the same group, you may want to integrate strategies like free writing, key words on the board, and direct textual reference in your discussion.

- Why do the Tectonic Theater Project cast members interview so many different people in Laramie?
- How many different views do we hear in the play?
- [Who] are the different constituencies represented in the play?
- Is it important to understanding the story that you hear so many different views of Matt and what happened that night?
- In what ways are the multiple viewpoints confusing?
- Whose story impacts you the most? Why?
- What is the significance of breaking the story into "moments"?
- In what ways do the Laramie community members characterize Matt Shepard's death?
- How is Matt characterized in the play? How does that characterization change depending on the person talking?

Continued on next page.

Box 5.5 continued

Faculty Guiding Questions for Discussion Groups at Student Opening Sessions
LaGuardia Community College

- What is the importance of the setting of the play?
- What does the play say about the role of religion in Laramie? In the United States?
- What does the play say about the role of class in Laramie? In the United States?
- What does the play say about the role of education and the university in Laramie? In the United States?
- What does the play say about the role of medicine in Laramie? In the United States?
- What does the play say about the role of the media throughout the crime and the trial?
- What is the significance of the "journal entries" in the play?
- What assumptions do people outside of Laramie make about the community? How is this expressed throughout the play?
- What does the play say about Laramie? About Wyoming? About the West? About the United States?
- Are there any "truths" in this play?
- Are there any redemptive moments in the play?
- Given the multiplicity of viewpoints portrayed in the play, what do you take away from reading the play?

Helpful Resources:
- Common Reading web site: http://www.lagcc.cuny.edu/laramie
- The Library of Congress' American Memory Collection has an extensive photography collection. You can download images or print them out. The site is at: http://memory.loc.gov/
- The Matthew Shepard Foundation is online at: http://www.matthewshepard.org/
- GLSEN: Gay, Lesbian, Straight Educator's Network provides lesson plans, topics for discussion, and pedagogical strategies. Their site is at: http://www.glsen.org/cgi-bin/iowa/home.html
- *Losing Matt Shepard,* a book of poems written in response to Matt's murder that Gail Green-Anderson brought to my attention
- Hate Crimes Legislation: The Gay and Lesbian Anti-Violence Project offers a useful overview on hate crimes at: http://www.lambda.org/hatecr1.htm#laws
- *The Universal Declaration of Human Rights* (1948) is available at the United Nations' web site at: http://www.un.org/Overview/rights.html

Conclusion

Events and activities are how common reading programs move from a solitary reading exercise to shared intellectual experiences. Events should be well organized and planned in advance to realize the goals and objectives of the common reading program. A variety of events gives students multiple opportunities to experience and discuss the book and related issues with teachers, peers, and other members of the campus community.

As with other aspects of the reading experience, planning and promoting activities should be an inclusive process. The "common" in common reading programs is best realized when students, faculty, and staff are all invested and engaged in the success of the program. Students should be encouraged and reminded, early and often, to read the book and participate in events. Reading promotes creativity and imagination so program planners should be creative and imaginative when designing and promoting activities.

Chapter Six

Using the Common Reading Selection in the Classroom

Many common reading programs are intended primarily as an orientation experience and do not intentionally seek to incorporate the reading into the classroom or curriculum. Other programs, however, aim to weave the selected book into various points in the curriculum—such as first-year seminars, writing classes, or general education requirements—and face the challenge of deliberately connecting the common reading program to the academic program. Connecting the common reading to the classroom advances several goals of such programs. It provides important opportunities for students' understanding of the academic expectations of college to be deepened and additional settings in which to enhance students' intellectual skills. Incorporating the reading selection(s) into the classroom provides further contexts in which students can reflect on and discuss what they read. Classroom activities designed around a common reading also facilitate community building through additional interactions between students and their peers and students and their teachers.

Faculty members are important partners in common reading programs and involving them in planning and implementation allows for more intentional inclusion of the common reading in their courses. Composition faculty and teachers involved with first-year seminars are obvious choices to facilitate the curricular component of a common reading program.

Connecting the Common Reading to the Academic Program

Many of the common reading programs described in this monograph incorporate the selected text into the academic program in some way. Using the book in the classroom may vary from integrating the book into the course curriculum and using it throughout the semester or quarter, or more simply setting aside a class period to talk about the book or the author's visit.

When a common reading is required for entering students, a logical place to discuss and write about the book is in a first-year seminar. Students in first-year seminars can attend common reading events as a class or in small groups, allowing for greater student interaction and engagement in academic experiences. In addition, if all students are enrolled in a first-year seminar, the common reading may be a required course text that is used across the term; thus, expanding it from a summer program to a shared classroom learning experience. Each year, Appalachian State University incorporates the common reading book into the first-year seminar curriculum. The book is also widely used in first-year English, and depending on the general topic of the reading, it may be used by faculty from other departments including political science, history, psychology, and geography.

Many reading programs aim to promote reading, writing, critical thinking, and other academic skills. The common reading text can be used to reinforce themes in the seminar and other courses and provide a context in which students can strengthen their spoken and written communication skills. At Temple University, the instructor for an Honors section of English composition incorporated the 2004 book, *Caucasia,* into the curriculum for the course. The theme for this composition class was "Identifying Writing," and instruction focused on recognizing features of good writing as well as discussing how identity in human beings is defined. The themes from *Caucasia* (i.e., race, families, identity) meshed nicely with the overall course goals and were a useful starting point for broader discussions of identity and how it is portrayed in literature. To promote writing, students were required to develop an essay using the writing prompt developed for the summer reading essay contest. Several students submitted their essays for the contest. To focus on speaking skills, students were asked to prepare questions for the author's visit and were encouraged to attend the author's main address to the university community (K. diNovi, personal communication, December 2004).

Learning communities are linked or clustered courses organized around a theme that enroll a common cohort of students and are an increasingly popular way to organize the curriculum, especially for first-year students. They offer interdisciplinary settings in which students can discuss or write about a common text from a variety of perspectives. Since many of the reading selections themselves are interdisciplinary, there is a natural connection between common reading programs and learning communities. Learning communities are also an ideal environment to promote community and the value of students learning from each other. At

Temple, about one third of all entering first-year students are enrolled in a learning community. Learning community faculty incorporate the common reading selection into their classes and across their communities in many different ways. When Temple students read *Fast Food Nation*, students in an education learning community explored a variety of issues—food safety, animal welfare, nutrition, and economics—from different disciplinary perspectives. In the history and English courses, students researched the history of food in Philadelphia and prepared presentations on topics such as the history of the Philadelphia cheese steak and the location of the first McDonalds in Philadelphia. In their first-year seminar class, they discussed and wrote about the pros and cons of selling fast food in public schools. They explored the economic, popular, cultural, and nutritional issues and prepared questions about these topics to ask the author during his visit to campus.

A common reading program can also support the goals of general education and the overall undergraduate degree program. The undergraduate program at St. John's College in Sante Fe, New Mexico, is a required course of study based on the great books of the Western tradition. Each summer, all students arriving at St. John's are required to read Homer's *Iliad*. Students are encouraged to read the book several times because as one college spokesperson notes, "…the more you read, the more familiar you are with the book, then the better able you will be to contribute to the discussion" (Crawford, 2003).

Teaching the Common Reading

Incorporating the common reading into the classroom requires applying basic principles of curriculum design: (a) what material will be covered, (b) what will students learn, and (c) how will teachers facilitate the learning process (Diamond, 1998). A distinguishing characteristic of common reading programs is that while the entire campus may read the same book, the content for discussions, assignments, and other activities around the book certainly does not need to be a one-size-fits-all lesson plan. Many books are selected because they offer many different ways and opportunities to teach and learn about a diverse range of topics.

Learning Goals

When a common reading text is incorporated into a course, there should be clearly defined outcomes for students—what should students learn or be able to do as a result of reading the book. This will help students understand what is expected of them and how their learning will be assessed. General goals for common reading programs might be closely aligned with the overall goals and skills for the course, which makes for a more natural incorporation of the selected book into a course (Box 6.1). If the primary goals for the course include enhancing students' critical thinking and discussion skills, then there should be classroom opportunities for students to interact with their peers and teachers and critically discuss what they

---

Box 6.1

Where Common Reading and Course Goals Converge

- Increasing students' motivation to read
- Improving students' reading skills
- Enhancing students' critical-thinking skills
- Promoting habits of discussion
- Increasing students' understanding of texts
- Improving students' ability to argue a position in a written assignment

---

read. Teachers should promote discussions that allow students to explore different perspectives, practice listening, and demonstrate respect for opposing viewpoints. Assignments and classroom activities should be designed to promote critical thinking and to provide students with feedback on their development. For example, students might be asked to develop an essay analyzing the ending of the selected text while simultaneously crafting alternative endings. To promote community and peer learning, students can share their endings with their classmates and work in pairs to edit and improve each other's work.

Among its many goals, the Common Reading Program at Gallaudet University aims to enhance students' reading and critical thinking skills. Guided reading questions are sent to students during the summer to help organize how they read and approach the book. The reading questions are designed using developmental reading approaches and are then incorporated into English classes. To promote critical-thinking skills, faculty who will be leading in- and out-of-class discussions with students are trained in discussion techniques that promote critical thinking. Campus Case 6.1 further describes how the common reading selection is incorporated into Gallaudet's first-year seminars and first-year English courses.

Pedagogy

Active learning strategies provide "opportunities for students to talk, listen, read, write, and reflect as they approach course content through problem-solving exercises, informal small groups, simulations, case studies, role playing, and other activities" (Meyers & Jones, 1993, p. xi). Such approaches can be used to incorporate a common reading into the classroom and contribute to the goals of common reading programs. Many of the books selected for common reading programs explore

Curricular Connections
Gallaudet University
Catherine Andersen

At Gallaudet University, the First-Year Seminar (FYS) course is required of all students. All seminars begin the semester with various assignments and activities centered on the selected book, and students receive credit for attending events related to the book.

Early in the semester, students discuss connections across themes from the New Student Convocation, the chosen book, and the University's Credo. An assignment in FYS requires students to meet campus community members through sharing buttons that say "I Read (Book Title)." Students approach others wearing the buttons and engage in informal conversations about the book's themes or what they liked or disliked about the selection. A mid-term writing project asks students to connect themes from the book to their own lives.

About one third of the seminar sections are included in linked-course learning communities. Seminars may be linked with English, biology, deaf studies, math, or history. Learning communities provide additional opportunities for interdisciplinary conversations about the selected book. Several communities design joint writing projects related to the book. For example, students in learning communities wrote an essay on their goals and sense of belonging after discussing a related experience and quote from the summer reading text.

Other academic programs require the book as well. The text is incorporated into developmental English classes and is required reading for new students participating in a Summer Bridge Program. In addition, many first-year English courses include the book in their curriculum. When essays about the summer reading were due in FYS, they worked on their first drafts in their English classes.

A goal of Gallaudet's Common Reading Program is to orient students to college-level critical-thinking and writing skills. This is accomplished in several ways. During the summer, students receive guided reading questions to help structure their approach to reading the book. Very specific developmental reading approaches are woven into the questions, which are then used to guide class discussion, particularly for students in developmental English classes. Staff at the campus tutoring center are available to help students who are having difficulty with the book.

In one developmental English class, students engage in collaborative learning exercises around the book. One lesson used for the 2004 Summer Reading selection, *The Pact*, asked students to relate the college experiences of the authors to issues they were facing in their own transition to college. One of the issues that the three doctors dealt with while in school was time management. Sam said, "I still liked to party too much and hadn't matured enough to realize that I couldn't hang out the same way anymore."

Students were divided into groups of three and wrote down possible suggestions to help any student deal with issues of time management. They then identified three other issues that new students confront and have to deal with in order to be successful. For each issue, they listed possible solutions.

Each group shared their issues and possible solutions with the class. The class discussed which ones would be most effective for different students and why. Problems and solutions were posted on the wall so students could refer back to them during the semester as they experienced problems.

Student responses on the *First-Year Initiative Survey* indicated that students feel the FYS helped them evaluate opinions and facts, and enhanced their ability to see multiple sides of an issue. Coordinators of the common reading program believe that it contributes to these positive results, and they are planning additional assessment to study the connections between the summer reading and critical-thinking skills.

multiple themes and raise many questions allowing readers to see the issues and plots in different ways. Teachers can move beyond a basic discussion in which they ask students to talk about what they liked or disliked about a reading selection and develop assignments or in-class activities that allow students to explore themes raised in the reading, practice important learning skills, and work collaboratively with their peers. Active learning strategies, including collaborative learning, discussion, and journal writing, are just some approaches that have been used by faculty to integrate a common reading assignment into their courses.

Cooperative or collaborative learning. "Cooperative learning is the instructional use of small groups so that students work together to maximize their own and each other's learning" (Johnson & Johnson, 1999, p. 5). Collaborative or cooperative learning promotes the related goals of helping students understand the assigned materials while also practicing learning with and from others, an important objective of many common reading programs. In small groups, students can discuss the content of the book, listen to each other's perspectives as they formulate answers to questions, and offer each other help and support in completing an assignment. Cooperative learning groups range from informal groups that spend a few minutes talking to each other about a question or issue raised by the teacher to more formal groups that work together for an entire class or over several class meetings (Johnson & Johnson). A more formal group might collaborate on a research project requiring them to write a paper and prepare a presentation on the historical period in which the selected reading takes place.

Debates are another collaborative learning activity that can help students explore a common reading in the classroom. Students are placed into groups to consider two positions—a pro and a con (Johnson & Johnson, 1999). Each group needs to reach consensus on their position and prepare an argument to defend their choice. The activity requires students to consider divergent viewpoints and to identify material from the selected reading to support their positions. When students in a first-year seminar class at Temple were required to read *Fast Food Nation*, they were divided into two groups to debate the economic and nutritional issues associated with selling fast food in public schools. Requiring each group to present their position(s) to the class also gave students the opportunity to strengthen their presentation skills.

Collaborative learning exercises are also an effective way to have students share their work with their peers. For the essay contest for *Caucasia,* Temple's 2004 reading selection, students were invited to write a piece describing where they saw the lead characters 10 years after the conclusion of the book. In one college composition course, students were assigned a character from the book and required to submit an essay on that character. Students were then placed into groups with other students who wrote on the same character. They shared their individual essays and were asked to agree upon, and share with the class, an epilogue for their assigned character.

Discussion. Brookfield and Preskill (1999) outline the benefits of discussion as a way of teaching. For example, discussion "teaches us dispositions and practices, provides us with the opportunity to serve and connect with others, and tests our ability to confront the most difficult of problems and think through them collaboratively" (Brookfield & Preskill, p. 20). Teachers can use questions, statements, and quotes to help generate discussion about the common reading. One activity Brookfield and Preskill suggest for generating discussion is a sentence completion exercise. Prompts that might be used for a common reading experience include:

> *What most struck me about the common reading book was….*
>
> *The character or subject in the common reading book that I most identify with is…*
>
> *The position in the common reading book that I most agree with is…*
>
> *The position in the common reading book that I most disagree with is…*
>
> *The question that I would most like to ask the author is…*
>
> *I think this book was selected for the common reading because…*

Students can also be invited to select and discuss a passage from the book that they particularly liked or disliked. In small groups or as a class, the students can share their reactions to the selected quotes or passages. Brookfield and Preskill suggest this approach addresses the common student concern that "subsequent conversation does not draw explicitly enough on the text they have been asked to spend time reading" (p. 73). Grounding discussions in specific passages from the text reminds students that an important part of the common reading experience is the careful reading of a book.

Discussion can also help students connect the reading to their own experiences. Students may be more likely to contribute to a discussion if it has personal meaning. Teachers can also invite students to share memorable experiences from their own lives that relate to themes in the common reading. A recent book selection for Bellevue Community College's BCC Reads project was *When the Emperor Was Divine* by Julie Otsuka. Students learned about the Japanese American experience during World War II not only from the experiences of the book's characters, but also from the collective family experiences and memories of their classmates (D. Douglas, personal communication, November 2004).

Journal writing. In describing the importance of the informal language of journals, Fulwiler (1987) notes that individuals

> find meaning in the world by exploring it through language—through their own easy talky language, not the language of textbook and teacher. Such language explorations may be oral as well as written, and are often expressed in language characterized as quite personal and colloquial. (p. 1)

Journal writing promotes several cognitive skills: observation, formulation of questions, speculation, self-awareness, digression, synthesis, and revision. For example, students can use journal entries to speculate about why an author chose a particular ending for a book or to analyze relationships between themes in the book and topics discussed in class. Other journal prompts might ask students to explore the relationships between characters, the personal relevance of issues to their own lives, or the historical context in which a book takes place. Such informal writing also allows students to be creative and expressive. Students can write a journal entry from the perspective of a particular character in the common reading or use their journals to record their responses to particular chapters or sections of a book.

When Temple students read *West of Kabul, East of New York,* the 2005 summer reading selection, those in one first-year seminar were asked to keep a journal reflecting on their views of world events. In particular, they were asked to write about their own ethnic backgrounds, their perceptions of the Muslim world, and their views on America's war against terrorism.

Making Use of General Resource Materials

Resource materials can also help students explore connections between the common reading program and surrounding areas or regional history. Students can use web sites to research background information for discussions or written assignments. When Temple students read *Lies My Teacher Told Me: Everything Your American History Textbook Got Wrong,* resource materials included a list of Philadelphia-area historical sites. In one first-year seminar class, students were assigned a group project in which they were required to visit an historical site—selected from the common reading resource list—and to prepare an oral presentation for the class.

Other helpful resources are book reviews, which can help students critically evaluate the selected reading. Links to book reviews can be included on the common reading web site or copies can be provided to students. Book reviews can also help frame discussion by inviting students to consider if they agree or disagree with a review. In class, students can be assigned the task of writing their own book reviews. Additional resource materials are discussed in chapter 5.

Conclusion

Connecting the common reading program to the classroom involves more than simply asking students: "What did you think of the book?" Just as out-of-class activities aim to promote student involvement, in-class activities should also promote student engagement with the material and each other. Faculty incorporating the reading into their classes should consider the types of active and collaborative forms of teaching and learning that can encourage students to explore the themes of the book with their peers. Program planners should develop resource materials to guide students and faculty in their reading and discussions.

The classroom activities for a common reading program need to be closely aligned with the goals for the program and the cocurricular activities in which students are also participating. By intentionally creating this relationship between the curricular and cocurricular components of the common reading program, the gap between students' in- and out-of-classroom learning is narrowed and learning is deepened. When the common reading is incorporated in the classroom, students not only gain knowledge and insight into what they are reading; but they also practice thinking, discussing, and writing about what they read.

Chapter Seven

Assessing Common Reading Programs

Catherine F. Andersen

Many entering students who participate in a common reading experience arrive on campus with their first assignment completed. They are often greeted by faculty, staff, and orientation leaders who are ready to engage them in discussion about a book. Related activities might include convocations featuring the author, discussion sessions, or essay contests. Entire courses may be designed around a common reading, or the book can become a central part of a first-year writing course, a first-year seminar, or the theme of a learning community. As reading programs increase and expand, institutions look to them to accomplish several goals, including enhancing academic readiness, increasing student engagement, and advancing institution-wide initiatives such as diversity. Common reading programs have the potential to impact all of these goals. As with any curricular or cocurricular program, assessment and evaluation should be part of an ongoing process that helps inform decisions about goals, intended outcomes, and allocation and justification of resources.

In a First-Year Assessment (FYA) Listserv posting, Cuseo (2000) hypothesized that a common reading program reproduces, on a smaller scale, the advantages associated with a core curriculum by providing a central learning experience that is shared by students. He continued by suggesting that

> ...the impact of a common reading experience on student learning may be magnified by multiple conversations students have about a common

reading experience, through formal faculty- or staff-led discussions, and spontaneous student-student conversations that may "spill over" to informal settings anywhere on campus. If such conversational synergy occurs, then two key theoretical principles of student retention and learning are likely to be implemented, namely: (a) active involvement (Astin, 1985), because these multiple conversations increase the amount of student time and level of student involvement invested in the learning experience, and (b) social integration (Tinto, 1975, 1993), because this common source of conversation promotes student interaction with other members of the college community serving to connect students with the institution and strengthen their sense of community membership.

While Cuseo (2000) made logical connections between common reading activities and theory, to hypothesize is not enough. Important questions to ask about common reading programs are "What kind of impact does this intellectual experience have on students and the community, and how can we document it?" This chapter discusses the definitions and purposes of assessment, characteristics of effective assessment, types of assessment, and potential outcomes. Examples of how various campuses assess their common reading programs are highlighted.

Definitions and Purposes of Assessment

Upcraft and Schuh (1996) suggest that while there is no consensus among experts as to the definition of assessment, it might be best defined as any effort to gather, analyze, or interpret evidence that describes institutional, divisional, or agency effectiveness. Assessment is a way of measuring and documenting whether something makes a difference. When choosing what to measure, program planners should assess something that matters and use assessment to help set priorities. For example, a survey of first-year students might reveal that they recommend continuing to mail students a copy of the summer reading, but that this practice had no impact on whether or not they read the book. Why should a program continue to send the book if funds are tight and could be used elsewhere? If, however, it was discovered that while the overall impact of sending the book was nil, further analysis indicated that for students receiving need-based scholarships it did make a difference, then the practice might continue. Assessment can offer the evidence that demonstrates the impact of a program or initiative and provides important information to guide improvement.

Purposes of Assessment

There are many reasons to assess common reading programs, including providing evidence demonstrating why the program should continue, justifying the expense of the program, and linking goals of the program to outcomes that measure student success. A well-crafted assessment of common reading activities can answer a variety of questions. A recent monograph, *Proving and Improving, Volume II: Tools and Techniques for Assessing the First College Year* (Swing, 2004), provides a wealth of information on assessing the first year of college and is a valuable source of information on assessment. The cover of the monograph depicts two students reading a document. Superimposed over this photo is a large microscope. Like seasoned sleuths, careful analysis of common reading programs can lead to proof that the program makes a difference and provide the necessary information to improve it.

Assessment can yield the necessary data to help answer questions in systematic ways. Upcraft (2005) states that

> assessment can and will demonstrate the effectiveness and worth of efforts to promote first-year student success and show positive relationships between students' participation in these efforts and curricular goals (such as content mastery, higher-order cognitive skills development, academic achievement, and persistence), as well as co-curricular goals (such as identity development, diversity awareness, social development, and spiritual development). (p. 473)

He continues by stating that truly effective assessment may include assessing important indicators such as cost-effectiveness; student satisfaction; student needs; policies and practices; and outcomes such as student learning, academic achievement, and persistence. Before any assessment is attempted, however, the qualities of effective assessment must be considered.

Characteristics of Effective Assessment

Regardless of what is measured and how, there are some fundamental characteristics that define effective assessment (Swing, 2004). According to Swing, effective assessment aspires to inform, change, or confirm existing practice. Successful assessment yields action either by guiding change or affirming the continuation of current educational strategies. He lists eight characteristics of effective assessment, all of which are relevant to the evaluation of a common reading program.

1. It focuses on what matters most.

High-quality assessment springs from an organization's well-defined goals, objectives, and mission. The question of what matters most in the assessment of a common reading program may vary from institution to institution, within the same institution from year to year, or may vary with the books selected. These may include logistical or fiscal concerns related to the program, learning outcomes, or outcomes that are connected to university-wide initiatives.

2. It focuses on elements that the organization can change.

Effective assessment should identify things we can change. One may not be able to change the fact that a living, best-selling author cannot be brought to campus for fiscal reasons. Also, one may not be able to change the fact that not all faculty can or want to participate in a common reading program or incorporate the text in their classes. What a program can change or influence might include the kind of book selected, who on campus becomes involved in the program, or the expansion of a successful pilot program.

3. It is built on the goodwill of participants and stakeholders.

Assessment efforts that are properly timed, orchestrated, and explained to participants are more likely to produce trustworthy data and outcomes. People who participate in a common reading program are more likely to be part of an assessment initiative if they feel their input is valued, and if it is done in a timely fashion requiring limited effort. When students, faculty, or staff are asked to provide input about the reading, it is important that they understand the purpose of the assessment and how their input will be used to improve the program. Having input in choosing next year's book may be good incentive to participate in a survey about the current year's reading.

4. It is multidimensional.

Assessment can produce credible results when information is established through corroborating studies using multiple measures and methods. To enhance the credibility of assessment efforts, the information gathered should be confirmed using a variety of sources. A survey administered right after a common reading program is completed could complement and support an end-of-the-year survey or first-year seminar course evaluation that asks students similar questions. Results of an instrument that uses benchmarking as a gauge might be triangulated with follow-up focus groups.

5. It includes input from all stakeholders.

When the assessment of a common reading program is initiated by those who run the program and have participated in it, the likelihood of assessing what really matters and what can be changed is increased. If senior administrators request information regarding the relative worth of the program, specific questions that are of interest to them should be asked. If continuation of the program is dependent on the relative cost versus the number of students who participate, or is tied to student outcomes such as a greater appreciation for diversity, this should be the focus of the evaluation. Those assessing the program need to consider what matters to the different stakeholders. The importance, however, of collecting information to help program leadership improve the common reading initiative should not be overlooked in efforts to meet the assessment mandates of others.

6. It places findings in an appropriate context.

Comparative benchmarks, longitudinal data, and/or professional judgments are needed to provide context for assessment findings. If, for example, results of longitudinal data or benchmarking indicate that students' out-of-class engagement or connections with faculty or peers are not of the quantity or quality desired, a common reading program might be implemented to improve student engagement. Student interaction with faculty and peers would then need to be assessed regularly to see if the common reading program improved the quantity and quality of student interactions with others. The benchmarking findings would allow for comparisons between programs, and when information is collected over a period of time, to indicate a particular program's progress.

7. It produces comprehensible results.

Reports should be written at the appropriate level of specificity for each target audience (e.g., executive summary, concise edition, full report). If a report is to be given to the provost who funded the activity, obviously the focus will be on how the funds were spent and who participated in such events. If the assessment was on strategies for increasing student participation, the data should be provided in a format that both students and faculty can access and understand.

8. It is disseminated and used.

Results must be shared with the individuals who shape the desired outcome, and decision makers should indicate how and when assessment data inform campus decisions. When individuals invest time and resources in a common reading program, they deserve timely feedback on their efforts. As soon as the results are in, the information should be widely disseminated. This is particularly important for a common reading program, for as soon as the event is over, it is time to select the reading and begin the programming for the following year. The University of South Carolina regularly assesses its first-year reading experience and results are shared with the planning committee. Campus Case 7.1 describes their assessment activities.

Types of Assessment

Once the outcomes have been identified, the type of assessment must be selected. Assessment can be conducted using quantitative methods such as surveys or data studies or qualitative approaches including student interviews, writing prompts, or focus groups. Quantitative data are used to find statistical relationships among variables, and qualitative data are used to find themes and non-statistical relationships among variables. Effective assessment, as described earlier in this chapter, makes use of multiple views and measures and is highly reliable when different tools are used to collect evidence.

Campus Case 7.1

Assessing Common Reading Programs
University of South Carolina
Carrie Linder

The University of South Carolina regularly assesses its First-Year Reading Experience for the purpose of improvement. Following the mid-August event, members of the program committee conduct a formal evaluation of the program. Three separate instruments are created and distributed to (a) discussion leaders, (b) student participants, and (c) students who did not participate. Evaluations ask students and discussion leaders to rate the book choice, resource materials, timeliness of information, keynote speaker, and their overall experience with their discussion group. Students who do not participate are asked to comment on their reasons for not participating. Until fall 2003, evaluations were mailed directly to discussion leaders and Honors students, but were distributed in class to University 101 (first-year seminar) students. Since fall 2003, evaluations have been conducted online.

To assess whether First-Year Reading Experience goals have been met, the committee analyzes student responses to the evaluations' open-ended questions and other questions that ask about student and faculty satisfaction with various components of the experience. Responses to statements such as, "Describe your understanding of the purpose of the First-Year Reading Experience," allow the committee to determine whether students truly understand the benefits of participating in a shared reading experience. Responses to statements such as, "Rate your experience in the small-group discussion" and "Rate the contribution of the faculty facilitator of your First-Year Reading Experience group," indicate whether students value the interactions with faculty and participation in college-level, academic discussions.

Feedback from the evaluations is compiled and distributed to members of the planning committee in early October. After results are shared with the committee and members have had an opportunity to provide their own feedback, decisions are made about aspects of the program that need to be altered to make it more effective or inclusive. As a result of lessons learned, the program has increased the number of students invited to attend each year, and in 2005, expanded to include the entire first-year class. Also, as a result of faculty feedback regarding their discomfort with leading discussions, the planning committee now writes and distributes discussion guides to all student participants and discussion leaders.

Survey Instruments

Quantitative assessment uses instruments that by nature of design provide data that are quantifiable or measurable. It is numerically based and can be analyzed using statistical techniques. Such information might include demographic data, pre-enrollment expectations, placement data, academic achievement data, or student satisfaction or participation data. There are a number of well-developed instruments designed for first-year assessment that measure some possible outcomes associated with common reading programs, such as involvement or satisfaction. Selected examples include the First-Year Initiative (FYI), the National Survey of Student Engagement (NSSE), the Cooperative Institutional Research Project (CIRP) Freshman Survey, and the Your First College Year (YFCY) Survey, which serves as a post-test to the CIRP Freshman Survey. Sometimes, these instruments may not provide relevant information. However, commercially prepared instruments often have space for institutions to provide supplemental questions. While participating in a national survey may be expensive, it may ultimately be more cost effective than local development, administration, and analysis of a survey. For example, a national survey may reduce the number of assessments needed by tapping into existing data collection and may allow data on common reading programs to be explained in a larger context.

Locally developed instruments, on the other hand, are useful in answering specific questions unique to the common reading initiative and of particular interest to the program or campus. Results can often be obtained more quickly since the instruments are scored locally, which is helpful if the program needs a quick snapshot of students' perceptions of the book or a common reading event. However, when tools are developed locally, the program should be prepared to answer questions about validity, reliability, and generalizability of the findings.

A program can also tie local assessment efforts to participation in national surveys. The Common Reading Program at LaGuardia Community College assesses its program through a survey administered at the Student Opening Sessions, the welcome event at which the book is featured. Surveys show that students continue to rank the faculty-led discussions as the most exciting part of the program. Results from the LaGuardia survey are then reviewed in the context of results on student satisfaction and engagement from the Community College Survey of Student Engagement (CCSSE) and the American College Testing (ACT) Opinion Surveys, which LaGuardia also administers to students.

Quantitative Assessment Methods

Swing (2004) suggests that there are four forms of quantitative assessment used in higher education: (a) criterion referenced, (b) value added, (c) benchmarking, and (d) prediction. Each can be used in the assessment of summer reading programs, but each approach has its limitations.

Criterion-referenced assessments. A criterion-referenced assessment structure uses a set score or number as the basis for "passing" or meeting a goal. For example, one might determine that, at a minimum, 50% of entering students must read the book before they arrive on campus to achieve a critical mass to discuss the text. Criterion-referenced assessments provide useful information, if the original "passing number" was selected for a sound reason. For example, if 55% of entering students read the book, but only 20% participated in follow-up discussion groups, are these events worthwhile? Suppose the 20% of the students who read the book and participated in the discussions volunteered to become discussion leaders in learning communities for the next fall? This event may then be defined as successful. Thus, while the criterion-referenced information provides some measurement, it has limitations. Swing (2004) states that these assessments are typically used to point out shortcomings of individual programs or achievement rather than to provide methods for improvement when the established goal is not met.

Value-added assessments. The I-E-O value-added assessment model was developed by Astin (1991) and uses the concept of input (what the student brings to college —entering characteristics), environment (in this case, the summer reading program), and outcomes (what happened as a result of the summer reading program). For example, it might be hypothesized that students who are conditional admits, those who did not meet the regular admissions standards, are more likely to read the book and demonstrate better academic skills (such as regularly completing assigned readings) if they receive it in the mail rather than being asked to purchase it on their own. The input is their conditional admissions status, the treatment is whether the book is mailed, and the outcome is whether they read the book or demonstrated any changes in academic behavior that can be attributed to reading the book. Did the program provide added value? While this model can be used to explore a variety of treatments and interactions, there must be strong evidence to suggest that the input and environment can explain the outcomes.

Benchmarking. Benchmarking is based on the premise that similar institutions can be compared to each other on a variety of outcomes. Because comparisons are made among like institutions, commercially produced instruments are often used. For example, instruments such as the First-Year Initiative (FYI), the National Survey of Student Engagement (NSSE), and Your First College Year (YFCY) provide opportunities for both institution-specific questions and access to a large database for comparison purposes. Benchmarking has been used in business and industry for some time but is now being used more frequently in colleges and universities. Benchmarking uses the value-added concept, but results are compared to similar institutions, and within the same institution, if used over time.

For example, suppose the intended outcome of the common reading program is to enhance faculty-student interactions and the initiative consists of multiple opportunities for interaction throughout the semester. At the end of the first semester, a commercial or national assessment tool is used to provide the necessary basis for comparison. Results indicate that faculty-student interactions are comparatively high for the institution that initiated the summer reading program as compared to similar colleges or universities that did not offer a summer reading. In this case, one might hypothesize that the result is directly related to the program and warrants further exploration. If there is longitudinal data, and everything else remained constant from previous years, it is possible to attribute this improvement to the common reading initiative. Another benefit is that by benchmarking against aspirant institutions, predictions about and support for potential programs might be justified (Swing, 2004). The biggest limitation of benchmarking is the cost of a commercial instrument, but this has to be weighed against the ability to compare outcomes to like institutions and the reliability of the assessment tool.

Prediction assessment. Prediction assessment is a variation of value-added assessment that makes use of a variety of statistical procedures to predict a specific outcome. Swing (2004) suggests that this module is frequently used to identify high-risk students before an undesirable outcome occurs. For example, common reading program leadership might predict, and later show, that those students who do not complete the required reading prior to arriving on campus are much more likely to be on academic probation at the end of the semester. Students who did not read the book could be identified early in the semester and carefully monitored for other kinds of academic behaviors that might lead to low achievement.

Qualitative Assessment Methods

While quantitative assessment uses numbers and statistics, qualitative assessment relies on verbal descriptions and comments. Qualitative assessment methods include interviews, observations, or document review (e.g., students' written material or presentations). Focus groups and interviews provide data in a social and interactive setting and, by design, may be more consistent with the goals of a common reading program, which often includes bringing students together for more meaningful interactions with peers. Siegel (2003) suggests that qualitative inquiry involves a process of discovery and analysis that provides a broader and deeper description of what is being studied.

Proving and Improving, Volume II (Swing, 2004) provides a number of excellent examples of qualitative assessments. One approach is the use of writing prompts. Students are given a prompt and a specific amount of time to free write on the assigned topic. For a common reading assignment, students might be asked to write about their perceptions of the book or why they think a particular book was selected. The writing submissions can then be analyzed for patterns. If the submissions are anonymous, students can be asked to provide demographic data—such as gender, ethnicity, residence, school, major, and course section—that can then be used to connect themes to possible sub-groups of students.

Swing (2004) suggests that both quantitative and qualitative assessment methods be used in evaluating a program. For example, if results of a survey indicate that a high percentage of female students did not like the selected book, a qualitative inquiry—such as interviews or focus groups with female students—might explain why women disliked the book.

Outcomes of Common Reading Programs

The most critical part of the assessment process is deciding on the kinds of questions to ask in order to collect the information that will be most useful to the program. For assessment purposes, intended outcomes need to be framed in terms of the information a program needs to demonstrate impact. Proving, through assessment, positive outcomes of common reading initiatives might ensure continuation or expansion of the program. A common reading program that can demonstrate achievement of intended program outcomes, as well as institution-wide outcomes, will get the attention of the campus community and may bring other first-year initiatives to the forefront as well.

Research questions should be closely aligned with outcomes for students, other participants, the program, the campus, or community. Cuseo (2000) suggests that there are three major domains that one can assess to demonstrate the impact of first-year initiatives on students. These domains include academic, personal, and specific forms and measures of development. Academic outcomes include academic skill development (e.g., program impact on writing and research skills), academic performance (e.g., program impact on participating students' GPA or on the percentage of students subsequently placed on academic probation), or student persistence to academic program or degree completion. Personal (holistic) development outcomes might include intellectual (e.g., critical thinking, intellectual curiosity), social (e.g., citizenship), emotional (e.g., self-esteem), or ethical (e.g., values clarification) outcomes. Specific forms or measures of development might include attitudinal (e.g., attitudes toward diversity), behavioral (e.g., incidence or frequency of participation in leadership activities), or cognitive (e.g., knowledge of the purpose and goals of liberal education) outcomes.

Using this categorization, research questions for common reading programs might include:

Academic

- Did reading the common reading book encourage students to read more?
- Did students who read the book score higher on a college reading test (pre and post) than students who did not read the book?
- Is there a relationship between self-selecting to read the book and first-semester GPA?
- Is there a relationship between participation in common reading program events and first-semester GPA?
- Did students who participated in the common reading program have higher scores on engagement measures as indicated by instruments such as the NSSE or YFCY than students who did not participate?

Personal Development Outcomes

- Did students seek additional information on issues raised in the book as a result of participating in the common reading program?

- Were students who read the book more likely to participate in civic activities as a result of the social issues raised in the reading than students who did not read the book?

- Were students more confident during their transition to college as a result of participating in the common reading project?

- If families were encouraged to read the summer book, did students whose family read the book report higher levels of family support?

- Was there any connection to declaring a major or choice of major and the content of the book selected?

Specific Forms/Measures of Development

- Was there any change in students' attitudes toward a theme (e.g., understanding of sexual orientation or diversity) that was emphasized in the book?

- Did students who participated in the common reading program participate in more community service activities than those who did not?

- Did participation in a common reading program enhance students' understanding of the academic expectations of college?

Assessment of the overall common reading initiative should also include questions that assess the impact of participation on faculty or other members of the campus community.

- How do faculty members perceive their involvement in the common reading program?

- To what extent was there campus-wide involvement in the common reading program?

- Did the common reading program increase overall campus awareness of first-year programs?

- Do faculty and staff feel more connected to students as a result of participating in discussions or events around the book?

- What were faculty opinions about the selected book?

Examples of Common Reading Assessments

Examples of ways other campuses assess their common reading initiatives can help other programs in planning their assessment and evaluation. However, while the experiences of other programs are helpful in designing assessment, assessment must be tailored to the student, faculty, and institutional contexts in which each common reading program operates.

At Appalachian State University, first-year students as well as faculty and staff who lead the discussions, are surveyed at the end of book discussion sessions. The results are used in planning the summer reading effort for the next year. Information collected allowed the program to conclude that the book selection criteria they set early in the process continues to hold true: that the length of the book matters; that the ability of the author to engage students is critical; and that the book needs to address timely topics, such as student transitions or world events.

At California Polytechnic State University, both students and discussion session facilitators are surveyed. A facilitator evaluation form is used to solicit feedback that includes information about the present year as well as suggestions for book selections for future years. In addition, a brief online survey is used to collect feedback from students. Students are asked to indicate the college in which they are enrolled allowing for analysis within these groups. Analysis can then guide the choice of a text. For example, is there wide variation by discipline as to how students perceive the selection? Do students in the business school respond less favorably to a particular text than those in liberal arts? If the goal is for a common reading, then the choice of a text would have to appeal to a wide audience.

Assessment should be linked to intended outcomes. At Gallaudet University, outcomes for the common reading program include:

1. Eighty percent of new students will read the book.

2. Through the common experience, new students will see the connection to one or more of the University's goals or initiatives.

3. The campus community will be involved in a common intellectual experience.

4. Students will want to read more.

5. Students will see the validity in others' points of view.

6. Students will view their own circumstances in relation to the book's theme.

The program is assessed through mid- and end-of-semester evaluations administered in the required first-year seminar. In addition, faculty and staff are invited to submit feedback. Past evaluations have revealed that a large percentage of students read the book (92% in 2003) and that the majority of students (61%) attended at least one out-of-class event. Students indicated that the reading program helped them prepare for the new semester and that the experience made them want to read more. After reading *Tuesdays With Morrie,* the 2003 selection, students reported that it deepened their appreciation for life, teachers, and their own family and friends. In their comments, faculty indicated that they have "never had students so enthusiastically discuss a book." Box 7.1 includes questions from the assessment used with this reading selection.

Temple University has annually expanded assessment of its summer reading program. In 2003, the author's visit and associated events were assessed using a comment card distributed at the author's main address to the University community. The pre-printed cards included questions about whether or not the participant read the book; why they attended the event (required, of interest, or both); and open-ended items about what they liked, disliked, or learned from the book or author's talk. The problem with the comment card approach was that information was only collected from students who were more likely to have read the book and have positive views of the common reading program than students who did not attend the author's talk.

In 2004, a web survey was designed to assess the program, book, and related events. The survey was aligned with the program's goals of (a) providing a common intellectual experience for entering students; (b) bringing students, faculty, and members of the Temple community together for discussion and debate; and (c) promoting cross-disciplinary thinking and dialogue in learning communities, first-year seminars, and other first-year courses where the text might be discussed. Box 7.2 lists questions used in the web survey.

Temple's survey provided concrete information about the program that could be used immediately, such as how to market the program, which events (required or not) were the best attended, and whether or not the book was discussed in any classes. The survey also asked a variety of questions that related to student engagement (e.g., Did students discuss the book with peers outside of class? Did students discuss the book with faculty in any of their classes?). The survey revealed that the majority of students who read the book did so because they understood it was expected of them and that most found out about the book during orientation or from a pre-semester mailing. Students commented that the 2004 book, *Caucasia* by Danzy Senna, was relevant to college students and that they would recommend this book to others. The popularity of this coming-of-age story, which also addressed family, gender, and race issues, led the summer reading committee to select "identity" as an overarching theme for future selections. The survey revealed that students did not have many opportunities to discuss the book in their first-semester classes. In response to this information, the associate director of the First-Year Writing Program was invited to join the summer reading committee; and in fall 2005, all first-year writing instructors received a copy of the selected book and were encouraged to incorporate it into their writing classes.

Box 7.1

Questions From a Mid-Semester First-Year Seminar Assessment
Gallaudet University

1. I read *Tuesdays With Morrie*.
2. I attended a *Tuesdays With Morrie* event.
3. I think the summer reading program is a good idea.
4. Reading this book made me want to read more.
5. I want more events like this.
6. After reading *Tuesdays With Morrie*, I…
   • Appreciated life more
   • Appreciated friends more
   • Appreciated family more
   • Appreciated teachers more
   • Did not like the book
   • Was more focused on academics
7. Reading this book helped me prepare for the first semester.

Note. Questions 1 and 2 are yes/no responses. Other questions use the following response scale: Strongly agree, agree, not sure, disagree, strongly disagree, or not applicable.

The Temple web survey also assessed the common reading events. In 2004, Temple piloted voluntary, summer reading discussion sessions. The sessions, called a "Book and a Bite," were held during breakfast, lunch, or dinner times at various on-campus dining locations. Sessions were lead by faculty volunteers. Attendance data showed that the evening sessions were the best attended, particularly when a residence assistant (RA) brought students from his or her floor. The survey revealed, however, that many students attended events only because they were required to for a class. To improve participation and interest in these discussion sessions, Temple is planning to move them into the residence halls and to work with RAs and hall directors to promote student interest and participation. Additional activities will be planned for commuting students.

Bowling Green State University (BGSU) initiated a summer reading program with a pilot project of 400 students in fall semester 2001 and expanded the program to more than 2,000 students by 2002. BGSU designed their summer reading project

Box 7.2

Sample Questions From an Online Common Reading Survey
Temple University

- Were you aware that all entering freshmen were asked to read *Caucasia* prior to the start of the semester?
- The primary reason I read *Caucasia* was…
- The primary reason I did not read *Caucasia* was…
- Did you participate in any of the summer reading events?
- The book is relevant to college students.
- The book touched on issues important to me.
- It was a book I could talk about with my friends.
- The book was reasonable in length for a summer reading.
- *Caucasia* is a book I would pick up on my own to read.
- The Freshman Summer Reading Project provided a common intellectual experience for my peers and me.
- Reading this book gave me something to talk about with students and teachers when I arrived on campus.
- This book made me think about issues not necessarily associated with my major or areas I plan to study.
- This book helped me explore ideas I might not have thought about.
- I would recommend this book to others.
- Was *Caucasia* a topic of discussion in any of your classes?
- Did you visit the Summer Reading web site?
- Are there any books you might suggest we consider for next year's Freshman Summer Reading selection?

Note. Most items were yes/no, Likert-scale, or open-ended responses. Students were asked to respond using a pull-down menu of response choices (e.g., strongly agree, agree, disagree, strongly disagree, not applicable) or to type comments into a text box.

and subsequent assessment around two major university-wide learning outcomes: "Connections" and "Participation." These objectives were then translated into the student outcomes they wished to measure. These included:

- To encourage students to read beyond what is required for a class

- To create a foundation for students to explore values and ethics

- To raise awareness and tolerance of intergenerational and cultural likenesses and differences

- To promote academic discourse and critical thinking

- To provide an introduction to the expectations of higher education

- To create a sense of community by increasing student-to-student and student-to-instructor interactions

- To integrate an academic and social experience into the campus community

Data was collected using a 22-item Student Discussion Questionnaire. Students who used the book in their first-year English classes were compared to those who did not. The study controlled for ACT scores, GPA, and demographic differences (e.g., race, gender, age). While the two pilot years produced somewhat different results, this assessment provided a wealth of information leading to further analysis. The evaluation of the 2001 Common Reading Experience pilot project included an open-ended opinion questionnaire that asked students directly about the reading selection, *Into the Forest* (Jean Hegland's tale of two young women coping in the aftermath of the apocalypse); what benefits they gained from reading the book; what events they attended when the author visited campus; whether they would recommend the Common Reading Experience to other students; and what book they would select. This opinion survey revealed that, on the whole, students responded quite positively to the pilot project. In fact, 79% of respondents recommended a common reading experience for first-year students in 2002.

Designing multiple assessments across years and book selections allows a campus to examine trends in responses and outcomes. For example, at BGSU, results of the 2001 pilot were more favorable than the 2002 results. Possible explanations included an all-day visit from the author of the 2001 selection as opposed to a lecture format used the following year. In addition, responses differed depending on the type of class in which the book was used. For example, students who read the book "for fun" as part of a University 101 course in which most students received an "A" gave more favorable responses than students who used the text as part of an English class. This may indicate that when "required" means asking students to engage in something solely for purposes of intellectual engagement and not for a grade, they may gain more from their participation.

Conclusion

Common reading programs may be only one component of first-year experience initiatives, but they have the potential to make a significant impact on students and institutions. Assessment studies this impact. Decisions about assessment should be part of the program planning process. Those responsible for planning assessment should start small and focus on what matters and on the things that can be changed. Assessment planning should involve stakeholders, use a multidimensional assessment approach, and connect results to the larger university context. Information and results should be disseminated widely. Limited resources or competing priorities may make assessment difficult, but small-scale assessments can be done using few resources. If campuses want to expand, improve, and sustain common reading programs, they cannot afford not to assess.

Chapter Eight

Conclusion: Going Beyond the Book

A theme throughout this monograph is that common reading programs are about more than just reading a book. Common reading initiatives are academic programs that should be well thought out with clearly defined goals and outcomes for all participants. The early chapters of this monograph describe typical goals and purposes for common reading programs and subsequent chapters address the elements necessary to create and sustain these efforts. This chapter summarizes and reiterates the major themes and issues involved in the work of building a common reading program, including recommendations for educators currently working in reading initiatives.

Phrases such as *student-centered, learning-centered, community-based, engagement,* and *involvement* are being used to describe work on many campuses that is aimed at deepening student learning, connecting students to their peers and teachers, building community, and enhancing first-year students' transition to college. Common reading programs bring students together with their peers, teachers, members of the campus community, and in some instances the greater community. By engaging in intellectual discussions around a selected book and its themes, students—particularly first-year students—can reflect on their personal beliefs, values, and experiences and take part in conversations that can deepen their learning across disciplines.

As repeated throughout this monograph, common reading programs are about bringing members of the campus together around intellectual matters. These programs send an important message that learning occurs not only inside the classroom but outside as well, and that a book can be "assigned" for broader purposes than meeting a class requirement.

Characteristics of Effective Programs

There is not a great deal of literature or research on common reading programs; however, they are often grounded in student success theory and in what educators consider best practice for nurturing students' intellectual and social development. In reviewing the existing literature on student success and examining common reading programs in place at various institutions, several characteristics of effective programs emerged.

Creating a common reading program provides a valuable opportunity for campuses to consider or revisit their goals and intended outcomes for students. Successful common reading programs are closely aligned with an institution's mission and priorities. When the common reading embodies values and goals shared across campus, there is typically greater support for the program and higher levels of participation. If a goal of the institution is to promote diversity, then a common reading program should aim to bring students together with faculty to engage in dialogue about a reading that raises issues of diversity (e.g., race, gender, ethnicity, sexual orientation).

Moreover, these goals are clearly articulated and guide decision making about the selection of the reading, related events, learning outcomes, and assessments. Goals for students might include encouraging reading, creating community, promoting discussion, or setting academic expectations. Faculty participation in reading programs can lead to greater interaction with students and colleagues from across campus. For the campus, goals might include creating dialogue about important and timely issues or promoting the institution's resources and programs to the larger community.

Common reading programs are often designed in concert with other efforts to enhance first-year student success such as orientation, first-year seminars, or learning communities. Common reading programs for first-year students typically begin during orientation when students are informed of the book, are asked to read it before the start of classes, and then participate in a variety of common reading activities. First-year seminars and learning communities are additional settings in which students can discuss, research, and write about themes in the book. Connecting common reading programs to existing first-year experience efforts provides a critical mass of participants to launch the initiative. Additionally, the program can be developed in the context of what a campus has already learned about what does and does not work in terms of academic programs, and organizers can bring new or renewed attention to existing efforts.

Common reading programs ask students to take a more active role in their learning and their intellectual transition to college. Because participation in common reading programs is frequently an expectation rather than a requirement, student willingness to read the book and take part in activities becomes a key factor in program success. Through their involvement in common reading programs, students can meet new people, relate their past experiences to their new roles as college learners, and explore ideas that they might not have readily considered independently. However, common reading programs that go beyond the book to create an impressive array of activities surrounding the reading selection are more likely to engage students. These successful programs include film series, art exhibits, library archives, contests, and other innovative events to deepen students' engagement with the book and interaction with each other.

Common reading programs set and model academic expectations for entering students. First-year students often comment that they are overwhelmed by the amount of reading they are expected to do in college. While common reading programs usually only involve one book that students read over the summer or an academic term, the reading initiative sends the message that reading and talking about what you read are central to student learning. Common reading programs demonstrate to students that learning is about both what and how you learn. Activities organized around the book can promote not only reading and discussion but also listening, public speaking, writing, research, respect for diverse viewpoints, and other important skills central to student success. Reading programs, by introducing students to faculty, administration, and staff, can also introduce students to the people and services available to support them in college.

Successful common reading programs are collaborative efforts of faculty, administrators, and staff from across campus. If a goal of the project is to connect students to faculty or incorporate a reading program within the general education curriculum, faculty members need to guide the book selection process and the planning of book-related events. If a common reading program is part of a broader initiative, first-year program leadership should invite faculty and colleagues from across campus to participate. Most book selection committees involve faculty, staff, and students and this enriches the selection process and leads to the selection of books that are interdisciplinary. Book-related events should be widely promoted and involve the broader campus community. Moreover, such broad-based partnerships lead to greater participation in activities and deeper support for the project and help ensure that the selected book is more likely to promote interdisciplinary ideas and allow for discussions that explore issues from different perspectives.

Successful common reading programs have moved beyond implementation and are institutionalized into their campus cultures. These programs grew steadily, cultivating buy-in and support as they expanded. Partnerships not only led to increased involvement across campus but also shared responsibility for funding the common reading initiative. These common reading programs are rituals recognized by the campus community as part of the transition to college for new students. Campus and local media often report the selection of the book and people regularly inquire, "What is the book this year?"

Successful programs use assessment to learn what did and did not work in terms of programming and why some book selections were more popular than others. Assessment is used for both "proving and improving" a program. In terms of accountability, successful programs use evidence to demonstrate that a program is meeting its goals, is contributing to broader campus priorities, and that continued or increased investment is justified. Perhaps more important, information is fed back into the program for purposes of planning and improvement so that students' experiences are enhanced from year to year, book to book.

Becoming More Than a Book Club

If common reading programs are to become more than just a reading project —a college student book club in which students read and minimally discuss a selected reading—they need to take steps to ensure the program is well-designed, supported, and assessed. First, the program needs the support and participation of senior leadership. When the chief academic and student affairs officers and others read the book, lead discussions, and attend common reading events, they provide important intellectual and community leadership for the project. Their involvement sends the message to students that they are joining a scholarly community.

Second, common reading programs need to move beyond orientation and connect to students' broader academic experiences. Extending a common reading beyond orientation and into the classroom provides students with sustained opportunities to discuss and write about what they read. Students are accustomed to "required" and "assigned" readings being part of their grade. When students invest time in reading a book, it is natural for them to want to demonstrate what they have learned. Extending the common reading program into the classroom and using the book across the curriculum, provides important opportunities for students to explore issues from different disciplinary perspectives and extends their learning beyond what is offered in the selected text.

Third, closely tied to the integration of a common reading into the curriculum or a general education program, is the importance of building and sustaining faculty participation. If common reading programs aim to introduce students to the academic expectations of college, it is important that students have the opportunity to practice habits of discourse with their teachers. If a reading is selected to reinforce themes or goals of a general education program, there should then be opportunities for students to discuss the reading in general education courses. Faculty members bring different disciplinary perspectives to the selected text and can help model the intellectual value of considering views different from one's own.

Common reading programs need to collect evidence demonstrating their impact on students, faculty, and the university community. Assessment needs to go beyond data on the percentages of students who read the book, participated in events, and whether and why they liked a particular choice. Most common reading programs have well-defined intellectual and social goals for students, and assessment needs to be aligned with those goals. Common reading programs need to demonstrate that reading a common book and participating in events with peers impacts how students learn, enhances important academic skills, and influences their attitudes and expectations of what it means to be a college student.

Finally, there is a need to build a larger literature base on common reading programs. This monograph is intended to be practitioner-oriented and to offer practical advice and useful examples on building and sustaining common reading programs. However, more research and literature is needed on how these programs are incorporated into the classroom and curriculum. Evidence-based literature is needed on how common reading programs impact student learning, skill development, involvement in the college experience, and personal growth.

Revisiting the Definition of a Common Reading Program

With the limited availability of published resources on common reading programs, a difficult task in preparing this monograph was coming up with a definition of "common reading programs." Throughout the monograph, common reading programs have been described as initiatives that engage a particular group of students, an entire campus, or possibly the neighboring community in the reading and discussion of a selected text or book. Having learned more about the experiences of several campus programs, the definition of a common reading program might best be categorized as a sum of all parts. All elements need to be present for the effort to succeed.

Common

Programs need to clearly articulate and disseminate the message that all students are expected to read the same book so they can participate in a shared intellectual experience and that members of the University community are invited to read the book and also take part in these activities. The "common," in the case of reading programs, does not mean students have a standard reaction to a book. Students read the same book so they can then contribute their individual perspectives, viewpoints, and experiences to discussions of the material.

Reading

One reason many campuses implement a common reading program is because they want to add a significant, academic component to orientation or the new student experience. Another reason is that they want to provide students with an opportunity to enhance their reading abilities and other intellectual skills such as listening and writing. Common reading programs also create community, and the reading is what brings faculty, students, and other members of the campus community together for a shared intellectual experience. The reading is the centerpiece for all involved.

Program

To be successful, a common reading initiative needs to be a program. A program has an administrative structure and dedicated resources. Successful programs have clearly defined goals, outcomes, and mechanisms for measuring progress in meeting these objectives. These programs are visible on campus and are recognized as an important part of the student experience and campus culture.

Final Advice

When colleagues reach out to educators on other campuses to learn more about their common reading programs, a first question is often, "What are you reading?" The book selections of many programs are listed throughout this monograph, and Appendix A provides a list of those books. Successful common reading programs have a structure and resources in place to support any selection. Enthusiasm for a book will vary from year to year, and some events will be better attended than others. What is important is that the reading initiative becomes an academic tradition. Leaders and planners of common reading programs need to pay as much attention to *how* students become engaged around what they read, as they pay to *what* students read. A successful common reading program goes beyond the book and provides meaningful opportunities for students to become integrated into a community of learners.

References

Astin, A. W. (1991). *Assessment for excellence.* New York: American Council on Education, Macmillian Publishing.

Barr, R. B., & Tagg, J. (1995, November/December). From teaching to learning: A new paradigm for undergraduate education. *Change,* 12-26.

Brookfield, S. D., & Preskill, S. (1999). *Discussion as a way of teaching.* San Francisco: Jossey-Bass.

Crawford, E. (2003, August 1). Reading and writing. *The Chronicle of Higher Education,* p. A6.

Cuseo, J. B. (2000). Assessment of the first-year experience: Six significant questions. *First-Year Listserv (FYA) Series.* [On-line serial]. Retrieved November 17, 2004, from http://www.brevard.edu/fyc/listserv/remarks/cuseo6000.htm

Diamond, R. M. (1998). *Designing and assessing courses and curricula.* San Francisco: Jossey-Bass.

Fulwiler, T. (1987). *The journal book.* Portsmouth, NH: Boynton/Cook.

Gardner, J. N., Upcraft, M. L., & Barefoot, B. O. (2005). Principles of good practice for the first college year and summary of recommendations. In M. L. Upcraft, J. N. Gardner, & B. O. Barefoot (Eds.), *Challenging and supporting the first-year student: A handbook for improving the first year of college* (pp. 515-524). San Francisco: Jossey-Bass.

Hartford Public Library. (2005). *One book for greater Hartford.* Retrieved on January 9, 2006, from http://onebookforgreaterhartford.org

Johnson, D. W., & Johnson, R. T. (1999). *Learning together and alone.* Boston: Allyn and Bacon.

Kuh, G. D. (2005). Student engagement in the first year of college. In M. L. Upcraft, J. N. Gardner, & B. O. Barefoot (Eds.), *Challenging and supporting the first-year student: A handbook for improving the first year of college* (pp. 86-107). San Francisco: Jossey-Bass.

Kuh, G. D., Douglas, K. B., Lund, J. P., & Ramin-Gyurnek, J. (1994). *Student learning outside the classroom: Transcending artificial boundaries* (ASHE-ERIC Higher Education Report No. 8). Washington, DC: The George Washington University, Clearinghouse on Higher Education.

Meyers, C., & Jones, T. B. (1993). *Promoting active learning.* San Francisco: Jossey-Bass.

Miami University of Ohio. (n.d.). *About the summer reading program.* Retrieved on January 9, 2006, from http://www.units.muohio.edu/srp/aboutsrp.html

National Survey of Student Engagement (NSSE). (2004). *Student engagement: Pathways to collegiate success 2004 annual survey results.* Bloomington, IN: Center for Postsecondary Research.

Patterson, L. (2002). New ideas in first-year reading programs from around the country. *First-Year Experience Newsletter (FYE), 14*(3), 8-9.

Rooney, M. (2003, April 25). Faith in books. *The Chronicle of Higher Education,* p. A8.

Saint Francis University. (n.d.). The goals of Franciscan higher education. Retrieved March 29, 2006, from http://www.francis.edu/about/Goals.shtm

Shapiro, N. S., & Levine, J. H. (1999). *Creating learning communities.* San Francisco: Jossey-Bass.

Siegel, M. J. (2003). *Primer on assessment in the first year of college.* Brevard, NC: Policy Center on the First Year of College.

Swing, R. L. (Ed.). (2004). *Proving and improving, Volume II: Tools and techniques for assessing the first college year* (Monograph No. 37). Columbia, SC: University of South Carolina, National Resource Center for The First-Year Experience and Students in Transition.

Temple University. (2005). *Freshman summer reading project.* Retrieved on January 9, 2006, from http://www.temple.edu/summerreading/

Temple University Libraries. (2005). *Freshman summer reading project [West of Kabul, East of New York].* Retrieved on January 9, 2006, from http://library.temple. edu/articles/subject_guides/freshmanread.jsp

Terenzini, P. T., Springer, L., Pascarella, E. T., & Nora, A. (1993). *Influences affecting the development of students' critical thinking skills.* Paper presented at the meeting of the Association for Institutional Research, New Orleans, LA. (ERIC Document Reproduction Service No. ED 372 666)

University of North Carolina at Chapel Hill (UNC) News Services. (2005, January 19). *Summer reading program selection committee picks 'Blood Done Sign My Name' for 2005.* Retrieved June 14, 2004, from http://www.unc.edu/news/archives/jan05/srp011905.html

Upcraft, M. L. (2005). Assessing the first year of college. In M. L. Upcraft, J. N. Gardner, & B. O. Barefoot (Eds.), *Challenging and supporting the first-year student: A handbook for improving the first year of college* (pp. 469-485). San Francisco: Jossey-Bass.

Upcraft, M. L., Gardner, J. N., & Barefoot, B. O. (Eds.). (2005). *Challenging and supporting the first-year student: A handbook for improving the first year of college.* San Francisco: Jossey-Bass.

Upcraft, M. L., & Schuh, J. H. (1996). *Assessment in student affairs.* San Francisco: Jossey-Bass.

Appendix A

Common Reading Texts
Referenced in the Monograph

Albom, M. (2002). *Tuesdays with Morrie.* New York: Broadway Books.

Anchebe, C. (1994). *Things fall apart.* New York: Anchor.

Ansary. T. (2003). *West of Kabul, east of New York.* New York: Picador.

Coelho, P. (1995). *The alchemist.* New York: Harper Collins.

Dog, M. C. (1991). *Lakota woman.* New York: Harper Perennial.

Edelman, M. W. (1992). *The measure of our success: Letter to my children and yours.* Boston: Beacon.

Ehrenreich, B. (2002). *Nickel and dimed.* New York: Owl Books.

Euripides. (1998). *Bacchae* (P. Woodruff, Trans.). Indianapolis, IN: Hackett.

Faulkner, W. (1958). *Three famous short novels: Spotted horses, old man, the bear.* New York: Vintage.

Fitzgerald, F. S. (2004). *The great Gatsby.* New York: Scribner Paperback Fiction.

Ford, R. (1996). *Independence day.* New York: Vintage.

Frayn, M. (2000). *Copenhagen.* New York: Anchor.

Frazier, I. (2001). *On the rez.* New York: Picador.

Gaines, E. J. (1997). *A lesson before dying.* New York: Vintage.

Gould, S. J. (1997). *Questioning the millennium: A rationalist's guide to a precisely arbitrary countdown.* New York: Random House.

Grooms, A. (2002). *Bombingham.* New York: Ballantine.

Hegland, J. (1998). *Into the forest.* New York: Dial Press Trade Paperback.

Hemingway, E. (1995). *The sun also rises.* New York: Scribner.

Hertsgaard, M. (2003). *The eagle's shadow: Why America fascinates and infuriates the world.* New York: Picador.

Hillerman, T. (1988). *A thief of time.* New York: Harper & Row.

Homer. (1998). *Iliad* (R. Fagles, Trans.). New York: Penguin Classics.

Hosseini, K. (2004). *The kite runner.* New York: Riverhead Trade.

Kotlowitz, A. (1992). *There are no children here.* New York: Anchor.

Lee, C. R. (2000). *A gesture life.* New York: Riverhead Trade.

Lee, G. (1991). *China boy.* New York: Plume.

Lipsky, D. (2004). *Absolutely American: Four years at West Point.* New York: Vintage.

Lowen, J. (1996). *Lies my teacher told me: Everything your American history textbook got wrong.* New York: Touchstone.

Mah, A. Y. (1997). *Falling leaves: The memoir of an unwanted Chinese daughter.* New York: Broadway Books.

Maraire, J. N. (1996). *Zenzele: A letter for my daughter.* New York: Dell.

McBride, J. (1996). *The color of water: A black's man tribute to his white mother.* New York: Riverhead Books.

McCrumb, S. (1994). *She walks these hills.* New York: Signet.

Mehta, G. (1997). *Snakes and ladders.* New York: Nan A. Talese/Doubleday.

O'Brien, T. (1998). *The things they carried.* New York: Broadway.

Otsuka, J. (2003). *When the emperor was divine.* New York: Anchor.

Ozeki, R. L. (1998). *My year of meats.* New York: Viking Penguin.

Patchett, A. (2002). *Bel canto.* New York: Harper Perennial.

Plotkin, Mark. (1993). *Tales of a shaman's apprentice: An ethnobotanist searches for new medicines in the Amazon rain forest.* New York: Viking Penguin.

Quinn, D. (1995). *Ishmael: An adventure of the mind and spirit.* New York: Bantam.

Roumain, J. (1978). *Masters of the dew.* Portsmouth, NH: Heinemann.

Russell, M. D. *The sparrow.* New York: Ballantine.

Salinger, J. D. (1991). *Catcher in the rye.* New York: Little, Brown.

Sanders, S. R. (1993). *The paradise of bombs.* Boston: Beacon.

Schlosser, E. (2002). *Fast food nation.* New York: Harper Perennial.

Sells, M. A. (1999). *Approaching the Qur'án: The early revelations.* Ashland, OR: White Cloud Press.

Senna, D. (1999). *Caucasia.* New York: Riverhead Books.

Shelley, M. (2004). *Frankenstein.* New York: Simon & Schuster.

Soyinka, W. (2004). *The Bacchae of Euripides: A communion rite.* New York: W. W. Norton.

Smith, A. D. (1993). *Fires in the mirror.* New York: Anchor.

Stoppard. T. (1994). *Arcadia.* London: Faber & Faber.

Suskind, R. (1999). *A hope in the unseen.* New York: Broadway.

Tyson, T. B. (2005). *Blood done sign my name.* New York: Three Rivers Press.

Appendix B

Summer Reading Book List

Each spring, the National Resource Center for The First-Year Experience and Students in Transition asks campuses with common reading programs to contribute the title of the texts(s) used by their programs. The list is maintained on the Center's web site: www.sc.edu/fye/resources/fyr/reading/read.html

The current list (as of June 2005) is provided below in alphabetical order by title.

Absolutely American: Four Years at West Point by David Lipsky
After Long Silence by Helen Fremont
Albright Court by Connie Rose Porter
Alicia: My Story by Alicia Appleman-Jurman
All But My Life: A Memoir by Gerda Weissman Klein
All Over But the Shoutin' by Rick Bragg
The American Dream: Stories from the Heart of Our Nation by Dan Rather
An American Story by Debra Dickerson
American Ways: A Guide for Foreigners in the United States by Gary Althen
Amistad by David Pesci
And the Waters Turned to Blood by Rodney Barker
Angela's Ashes: A Memoir by Frank McCourt
Antigone by Sophocles
Anti-Semite and Jew: An Exploration of the Etiology of Hate by Sartre
Approaching the Qur'án: The Early Revelations by Michael Sells
Arcadia by Tom Stoppard
Atonement by Ian McEwan
Auden and the Liposome by Gerald Weissman
Autobiography of a Face by Lucy Grealy
The Bacchae by Euripides
Badenheim 1939 by Aharon Appelfeld
The Beak of the Finch: A Story of Evolution in Our Time by Nathan Weiner
The Bear by William Faulkner
Beloved by Toni Morrison
The Big Random by Dana Yeaton
Black Dog of Fate by Peter Balakian
Black Ice by Lorene Carey
Brave New World by Aldous Huxley

Brighten the Corner Where You Are: A Novel by Fred Chappell

Buck v. Bell, 274 U.S. 200; 47 S. Ct. 584. (Supreme Court Case)

Can Animals and Machines Be Persons: A Dialogue by Justin Leiber

Carrie Buck's Daughter by Stephen Jay Gould

Catch 22 by Joseph Heller

Catcher in the Rye by J.D. Salinger

China Boy by Gus Lee

Choice by Annaliese Hood

The Chosen by Chaim Potok

Chronicle of a Death Foretold by Gabriel Garcia Marquez

Clay's Quilt by Silas House

Cold Mountain by Charles Frazier

The Color of Water: A Black Man's Tribute to His White Mother by James McBride

Colored People by Henry Louis Gates, Jr.

Coming of Age in Mississippi by Anne Moody

Confederates in the Attic: Dispatches from the Unfinished Civil War by Tony Horwitz

Copenhagen by Michael Frayn

A Correspondence Course by Nadine Gordimer

Days of Grace by Arnold Rampersad

Dead Man Walking by Sister Helen Prejean

A Delusion of Satan: The Full Story of the Salem Witch Trials by Frances Hill

Democracy's Discontent: America in Search of a Public Philosophy by Michael Sandel

The Demon-Haunted World: Science as a Candle in the Dark by Carl Sagan

Disturbing the Universe by Freeman Dyson

Due Preparations for the Plague by Janette Turner Hospital

E=MC2: A Biography of the World's Most Famous Equation by David Bodanis

Einstein's Dreams by Alan Lightman

Endurance: Shackleton's Incredible Voyage by Alfred Lansing

The Endurance: Shackleton's Legendary Antarctic Expedition by Caroline Alexander

Fair and Tender Ladies by Lee Smith

Farewell, I'm Bound to Leave You by Fred Chappel

Fast Food Nation by Eric Schlosser

A Father's Story by Andre Dubus

The Final Forest: The Battle for the Last Great Trees of the Pacific Northwest by William Dietrich

Finding Fish: A Memoir by Antwone Fisher

Fires in the Mirror: Crown Heights, Brooklyn and Other Identities by Anna Deavere Smith

The Flawed Path to the Presidency 1992: Unfairness and Inequality in the Presidential Selection Process by Robert Loevy

Flunk the Gene Test and Lose Your Insurance by Geoffrey Cowley

Fortunate Son: The Autobiography of Lewis B. Puller, Jr. by Lewis Puller

Frankenstein by Mary Shelley

Friday Night Lights: A Town, A Team, and a Dream by H. G. Bissinger

Fried Green Tomatoes at the Whistlestop Cafe by Fannie Flagg

The Gangster We Are All Looking For by Le Thi Diem Thuy
Gap Creek by Robert Morgan
Girl with a Pearl Earring by Tracy Chevalier
God and Mammon in America by Robert W. Wuthnow
A Gracious Plenty by Sheri Reynolds
Granny D: You're Never Too Old to Raise a Little Hell by Doris Haddock
Grizzly Years: In Search of the American Wilderness by Doug Peacock
Guns, Germs, and Steel: The Fates of Human Societies by Jared Diamond
The Hard Questions by Jean Bethke Elshtain
Harry Potter and the Order of the Phoenix by J. K. Rowling
Harry Potter and the Sorcerer's Stone by J. K. Rowling
Haven: The Dramatic Story of 1,000 World War II Refugees and How They Came to America by Ruth Gruber
Having Our Say by Sarah L. Delany, A. Elizabeth Delany with Amy Hill Hearth
Henry Ford by Italo Calvino
Honest Effort by Michael Carey
Honky by Dalton Conley
A Hope in the Unseen by Ron Suskind
The House on Mango Street by Sandra Cisneros
How We Die by Sherwin Nuland
Hunger of Memory: The Education of Richard Rodriguez by Richard Rodriguez
I Am One of You Forever: A Novel by Fred Chappel
I Know Why the Caged Bird Sings by Maya Angelou
The Immigration Dilemma: Avoiding the Tragedy of the Commons by Garrett Hardin
In A Different Voice: Psychological Theory and Women's Development by Carol Gilligan
In Country by Bobbie Ann Mason
In the Time of the Butterflies by Julia Alvarez
Infinite in All Directions: Gifford Lectures Given at Aberdeen, Scotland April-November 1985 by Freeman Dyson
Inherit the Wind by Jerome Lawrence and Robert E. Lee
Interpreter of Maladies by Jhumpa Lahiri
Into the Forest by Jean Hegland
Into the Wild by Jon Krakauer
Into Thin Air: A Personal Account of the Mount Everest Disaster by Jon Krakauer
Ishmael: An Adventure of the Mind and Spirit by Daniel Quinn
It's Not About the Bike: My Journey Back To Life by Lance Armstrong
John Henry Days by Colson Whitehead
The Joy Luck Club by Amy Tan
Keys to the City: Tales of a New York City Locksmith by Joel Kostman
Kindred by Octavia Butler
The Laramie Project by Moises Kaufman
The Left Hand of Darkness by Ursula LeGuin
A Lesson Before Dying by Ernest Gaines
Letters from Yellowstone by Diane Smith

The Lexus and the Olive Tree by Thomas Friedman

Lies My Teacher Told Me by James W. Loewen

Life of Pi by Yann Martell

Life on the Color Line: The True Story of a White Boy Who Discovered He Was Black by Gregory Williams

Lincoln at Gettysburg: The Words that Remade America by Gary Wills

Little Lamb, Who Made Thee? by Sharon Begley

Lolita by Vladimir Nabokov

Lone Ranger and Tonto: Fistfight in Heaven by Sherman Alexie

The Long Walk by Slavomir Rawicz

Lost in Translation: A Life in a New Language by Eva Hoffman

Lying: Moral Choice in Public and Private Life by Sissela Bok

Mad River Rising: A Play in Two Acts by Dana Yeaton

Makes Me Wanna Holler: A Young Black Man in America by Nathan McCall

Major Barbara by George Bernard Shaw

A Man For All Seasons by Robert Bolt

A Map of the World by Jane Hamilton

Men Are From Mars, Women Are From Venus by John Gray

The Metamorphosis by Franz Kafka

Middle Passages by Charles Johnson

Midwives: A Play by Dana Yeaton

A Midwife's Story by Penny Armstrong and Sheryl Feldman

The Mismeasure of Man by Stephen Jay Gould

Migrations of the Heart: An Autobiography by Marita Golden

The Milagro Beanfield War by John Nichols

A Moveable Feast by Ernest Hemingway

Music as Medicine by Deforia Lane

"My Life as a Move" from *Into Woods* by Bill Roorbach

My Own Country by Abraham Vergehese

My Year of Meats by Ruth Ozeki

Naked in Baghdad by Ann Garrels

Narrative of the Life of Frederick Douglass by Frederick Douglass

Native Speaker by Chang-Rae Lee

Nickel and Dimed: On (Not) Getting by in America by Barbara Ehrenreich

Night by Elie Wiesel

"Of the Wings of Atalanata" by W.E.B. DuBois

The Ones Who Walk Away From Omelas by Ursula LeGuin

October Sky by Homer Hickam

On Liberty by John Stuart Mill

Oral History by Lee Smith

Ordinary Grace: An Examination of the Roots of Compassion, Altruism, and Empathy, and the Ordinary Individuals who Help Others in Extraordinary Ways by Kathleen Brehony

The Other Side of the River: A Story of Two Towns, a Death, and America's Dilemma by Alex Kotlowitz

The Pact: Three Young Men Make a Promise and Fulfill a Dream by Sampson Davis, George Jenkins, Rameck Hunt, and Lisa Frazier Page

The Paradise of Bombs by Scott R. Sanders

Parental Origin of Chromosome May Determine Social Graces, Scientists Say by Natalie Paul Angier

Plainsong by Kent Haruf

Ragtime by E. L. Doctorow

Rashomon and Other Stories by Ryunosuke Akutagawa

Reading Lolita in Tehran: A Memoir in Books by Azar Nafisi

Refuge by Terry Tempest Williams

Respect by Sara Lawrence Lightfoot

Reviving Ophelia: Saving the Selves of Adolescent Girls by Mary Pipher

The Road From Coorain by Jill Ker Conway

Rocket Boys by Homer Hickam

Running Tide by Joan Benoit Samuelson

The Samurai's Garden by Gail Tsukiyama

Savage Inequalities by Jonathan Kozol

Separation of Powers: Does it Still Work? by R. Goldwin (Ed.)

Seven Habits of Highly Effective People by Stephen Covey

She Walks These Hills by Sharyn McCrumb

The Sky Unwashed by Irene Zabytko

Snow Falling on Cedars by David Guterson

Sounds of the River: A Young Man's University Days in Beijing by Da Chen

The Sparrow by Mary Doria Russell

The Spirit Catches You and You Fall Down by Anne Fadiman

Take the Cannoli by Sarah Vowell

Tales of a Shaman's Apprentice: An Ethnobotanist Searches for New Medicines in the Rainforest by Mark Plotkin

Tell Them Who I Am by Elliot Liebow

There Are No Children Here: The Story of Two Boys Growing Up in the Other America by Alex Kotlowitz

Things Fall Apart by Chinua Achebe

The Things They Carried by Tim O'Brien

The Tipping Point: How Little Things Can Make a Big Difference by Malcolm Gladwell

To Form a Government by Lloyd Cutler

Tom and Huck Don't Live Here Anymore: Childhood and Murder in the Heart of America by Ron Powers

Tom Sawyer by Mark Twain

Tuesdays With Morrie by Mitch Albom

The Truest Pleasure by Robert Morgan

The Twenty-First Century by Freeman Dyson

Typical American by Jen Gish

Two Old Women by Velma Wallis

The United States Constitution

Wait Till Next Year: A Memoir by Doris Kearns Goodwin

Waiting for the Barbarians by J. Coetzce

Water Witches by Chris Bohjalian

We Wish to Inform You That Tomorrow We Will Be Killed With Our Families: Stories From Rwanda by Philip Gourevitch

West of Kabul, East of New York: An Afghan American by Tamim Ansary

When Bad Things Happen to Good People by Harold S. Kushner

When the Emperor Was Divine by Julie Otsuka

When I Was Puerto Rican by Esmeralda Santiago

When Virtue Loses All Her Loveliness, Some Reflections on Capitalism and the Free Society by Irving Kristol

Where the Buffalo Roam by Anne Matthews

Where the Rivers Flow North by Howard Frank Mosher

Whisper of the River by Ferrol Sams

White Noise by Don DeLillo

Whiz Kids by Stephen Covey

The Wisdom of Repugnance by Leon R. Kass

Wolf Wars by Hank Fischer

Woman Warrior by Maxine Hong Kingston

Work and Play by Michael Oakeshott

Yellow Raft in Blue Water by Michael Dorris

About the Authors

Jodi Levine Laufgraben has worked at Temple University in various capacities for 16 years. She is presently the associate vice provost and director of periodic program review. In this position, she manages program review and accreditation activities for the Office of the Provost. Prior to this position, she served as assistant vice provost for university studies, where she developed and directed several academic programs aimed at improving undergraduate teaching and learning including learning communities, a first-year seminar, and the Freshman Summer Reading Project. She was a principal investigator in the Restructuring for Urban Student Success Project, was a fellow for the National Learning Communities Project, and is active in the Northeast Region Learning Communities Fellows Group. She is a past member of the National Advisory Board for the National Resource Center for The First-Year Experience and Students in Transition, and in 2001-2002 she was a member of the Middle States Commission on Higher Education's Advisory Panel on Student Learning and Assessment that assisted in the development of the 2003 publication *Student Learning Assessment*. In addition to her administrative responsibilities, Levine Laufgraben is an instructor in Educational Leadership and Policy Studies, teaching courses on educational administration, research design, action and collaborative research, planning, and personnel. Her publications include *Sustaining and Improving Learning Communities* and *Creating Learning Communities* (both co-authored with Nancy Shapiro) and the monograph *Learning Communities: New Structures, New Partnerships for Learning*.

Catherine Andersen is director of the First Year Experience at Gallaudet University in Washington, D.C. In her tenure at Gallaudet, she has served as a department chair, special assistant to the vice president of academic affairs, director of orientation and retention, interim associate dean and interim director of developmental studies. In 1994, she was the recipient of Gallaudet University's Distinguished Faculty of the Year; and in 1997, she was recognized as an Outstanding First-Year Student Advocate by the National Resource Center on The First-Year Experience and Students in Transition. In 2004, she was appointed to the National Advisory Board for the National Resource Center. In 1999, under her direction, the First Year Experience Program at Gallaudet received a four-year grant from The Mellon Foundation to infuse technology into the first-year seminar. Andersen has appeared in national teleconferences on assessing first-year seminars (2003) and creating campus cultures for student success (2006) and has presented at more than 30 national and international conferences. She has served as an editor and primary author on a number of monographs related to postsecondary students. Her current interests include the role of emotional intelligence in the first year of college.

Christopher Dennis serves as associate vice provost for undergraduate studies at Temple University, working on policy and curriculum development and redesign of the general education program. His academic specialty is Medieval and Renaissance Studies, and he has taught literature and writing at Princeton University, the University of Michigan, the University of Pennsylvania, and the University of London. Dennis was formerly the executive director of academic programs in residence, director of college house programs, and acting director of residential living at the University of Pennsylvania. He joined the faculty at Temple in 1999 and teaches in the English department, Honors Program, and the Intellectual Heritage Program. He received his B.A. from the University of Massachusetts, M.A. from Oxford University, and Ph.D. from Princeton University.